General Editors: J. R. MULRYNE
and J. C. BULMAN
Associate Editor: Margaret Shewring

The Taming of the Shrew

Already published in the series

J. L. Styan   *All's Well that Ends Well*
Jill Levenson   *Romeo and Juliet*
Roger Warren   *Cymbeline*

In production

Hugh Richmond   *Richard III*
Alan Dessen   *Titus Andronicus*
J. R. Mulryne   *Antony and Cleopatra*
J. C. Bulman   *The Merchant of Venice*
Margaret Shewring   *Richard II*
Alexander Leggatt   *King Lear*
Carol Rutter   *Henry VI*
Roger Savage   *The Tempest*
Miriam Gilbert   *Love's Labour's Lost*

Volumes on most other plays in preparation

Of related interest

J. L. Halio   *Understanding Shakespeare's plays in performance*

The Taming
of the Shrew

GRAHAM HOLDERNESS

Manchester
University Press

Manchester and New York

Distributed exclusively in the USA and Canada by St. Martin's Press

Published by
Manchester University Press

Oxford Road, Manchester, M13 9PL
and Room 400, 175 Fifth Avenue,
New York, NY 10010, USA

Distributed exclusively in the USA and Canada
by St. Martin's Press, Room 400, 175 Fifth Avenue,
New York, NY 10010, USA

British Library cataloguing in publication data
Holderness, Graham
    The taming of the shrew. – (Shakespeare in performance).
    1. Drama in English. Shakespeare, William, 1564-1616
    Taming of the shrew. Performance
    I. Title II. Series
    792.9'5

Library of Congress cataloging in publication data applied for
Holderness, Graham.
    The Taming of the Shrew.
    (Shakespeare in performance)
    Bibliography: p.
    Includes index.
    1. Shakespeare, William, 1564-1616. Taming of the Shrew.
    2. Shakespeare, William, 1564-1616—Stage history.
    I. Shakespeare, William, 1564-1616. Taming of the Shrew.
    II. Title. III. Series.
    PR2832.H65   1989   822.3'3   88-32644
    ISBN 0-7190-2737-3

ISBN 0 7190 2737 3 *hardback*

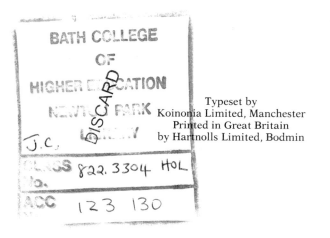
Typeset by
Koinonia Limited, Manchester
Printed in Great Britain
by Hartnolls Limited, Bodmin

CONTENTS

The illustrations appear between chapters III and IV, pp. 72, 73

For Marilyn

SERIES EDITORS' PREFACE

The study of Shakespeare's plays as scripts for performance in the theatre has grown in recent years to become a major interest for many university, college and secondary-school students and their teachers. The aim of the present series is to assist this study by describing how certain of Shakespeare's texts have been realised in production.

The series is not concerned to provide theatre histories. Rather, each contributor has selected a small number of productions of a particular play and studied them comparatively. The productions, often from different periods, countries and media, have been chosen because they are significant interpretations in their own right, but also because they represent something of the range and variety of possible interpretations of the play in hand. We hope that students and theatregoers, by reading these accounts of Shakespeare in performance, may enlarge their understanding of the text and begin, too, to appreciate some of the ways in which practical considerations influence the meanings a production incorporates: the stage the actor plays on, the acting company, the player's own physique and abilities, stage-design and theatre-tradition, as well as the political, social and economic conditions of performance and the expectations of a particular audience.

Any study of a Shakespeare text will reveal only a small proportion of the text's potential meaning. We hope that the effect of this series will be to encourage a kind of reading that is receptive to the ever-varying discoveries theatre interpretation provides.

J. R. Mulryne
J. C. Bulman
Margaret Shewring

[vii]

ACKNOWLEDGMENTS

Some of the arguments and explanations to be found in this book have been presented in the form of conference papers: and I am grateful, for attention, appreciation and criticism, to participants in the University of Wales Staff Colloquium on *History and Literature*, University College of Swansea, May, 1987; and to those attending the conference on *Frau, Macht und Humanität bei Shakespeare*, organised by the Deutsche Shakespeare-Gesellshaft, and held in Weimar in 1987. The latter paper, incorporating some of the material on Bogdanov and Miller here first published in English, was published in German in *Shakespeare Jahrbuch*, 124, 1988, pp. 101-8. Passages of the section on Jonathan Miller's 1988 Royal Shakespeare Company production of *The Taming of the Shrew* (see pp. 118-20) appeared in 'The Albatross and the Swan: two productions at Stratford', in *New Theatre Quarterly*, 14, 1988, pp. 152-8. I have made extensive use of research material kindly provided to me by my colleagues Christopher J. McCullough and Robert Shaughnessy; and I have purloined ideas offered to me by my colleagues Susanne Greenhalgh and Valerie Taylor. The General Editors of the series, Ronnie Mulryne and Jim Bulman, provided invaluable advice and constructive criticism.

For permission to reproduce illustrations, I am grateful to Joe Cocks Studio, Angus Bean, Laurence Burns and the Shakespeare Birthplace Trust.

CHAPTER I

Introduction

I Two Shrews

Anyone present at a performance of Shakespeare's *The Taming of the Shrew* in Britain at any time since 1913 is quite likely to have witnessed a hybrid amalgamation of two discrete play-texts: the text contained in the First Folio of 1623, which we accept as Shakespeare's play *The Taming of the Shrew*; and the anonymous play known as *The Taming of a Shrew*, printed in 1594, which was once held to be a source of Shakespeare's play, but is now regarded by most scholars as a 'memorial reconstruction' of a Shakespearean original.[1]

Shakespeare's play in the form we have inherited it contains of Christopher Sly only the two opening scenes known as the 'Induction': from the opening of the *Shrew* action, nothing more is seen or heard of the dreaming, drunken tinker. In *The Taming of a Shrew*, by contrast, the Sly-narrative is not a prologue but an extended dramatic framework: Sly and his attendants are kept on stage more or less throughout, and are given several further comments on and interventions in the action of the play. This sustained presence of the choric observer is more in keeping with contemporary stage practice, as exemplified in plays such as Kyd's *The Spanish Tragedy*, Greene and Lodge's *A Looking Glass for London and England*, and Greene's *James IV*.[2] Even a short introductory chorus like that of Marlowe's *Dr Faustus* would be expected at least to reappear as an epilogue: and the 'induction' to *The Taming of the Shrew* seems far too elaborate and promising a theatrical invention to be simply abandoned or dropped out of sight.

Even the two-scene 'Induction' disappeared from the play for centuries while Garrick's *Catherine and Petruchio* and other adaptations held the stage: in 1900 Frank Benson was still producing the play with no trace of Christopher Sly. Subsequent directors such as Oscar Asche (1904), W. Bridges Adams (1933) and F. Owen Chambers (1936) restored the 'Induction', but often in a cut form. It was Martin Harvey, acting under the advice and influence of William Poel, who in a 1913 production at the Prince of Wales Theatre, decided to supplement Shakespeare's text by interpolating the Christopher Sly scenes from *A Shrew*: and to develop the Sly-framework into a constitutive element of the drama. In this and many subsequent productions, Sly and his attendants were kept on stage, where they functioned as a surrogate audience: in accordance with the Lord's directions, the actors involved in the *Shrew* narrative constantly referred and deferred to them as the privileged audience of their presentation. Directors would give Sly lines which belong in the Shakespearean text to other characters: e.g. Tranio's observation (I.i.169) 'That wench is stark mad, or wonderful forward' became, in Theodore Komisarjevsky's 1939 Stratford production, a spectator's observation from outside the dramatic event. In the same production Sly made several abortive attempts to intervene in the action in the manner of Beaumont's intrusive grocer in *The Knight of the Burning Pestle*: at several points he tried to join the actors in the *Shrew* narrative, and had to be forcibly restrained by the Page.[3]

Since Martin Harvey's pioneering production, the Christopher Sly framework has been embraced by the modern theatre with particular enthusiasm: to such an extent that it became commonplace to augment the play in performance with the Sly interventions and epilogue preserved in the 1594 Quarto text.[4] Traditionally, modern edited texts of Shakespeare's plays have been constructed by collating the various available early texts, amalgamating and synthesising, or discriminating between different 'readings'. 'Good' Quarto texts (those thought to have been published with some kind of authorisation from Shakespeare and his company) are judged as reliable, as records of Shakespeare's intentions, as the texts printed in the Folio. Even 'bad' Quarto texts are

[2]

regarded by modern textual scholars as useful sources of information about the plays in performance. Nonetheless, within the dominant discourses of literary criticism and textual scholarship, the relation between, on the one hand, a 'good' text like that of the Folio, or that of a 'good' Quarto, and on the other, that of a so-called 'bad' Quarto, is clear: the latter is an inferior, garbled version of the authorial intention faithfully preserved in the former.

Once *The Taming of a Shrew* was acknowledged by editors as a corrupted version of Shakespeare's play, that is, as a 'bad' Quarto, rather than as a source-play or an early draft, then it came within the orbit of editorial interest, and could be referred to in the composition of a scholarly edition of *The Taming of the Shrew*. Although the play's authorship, or at least its ancestry, could therefore be traced ultimately to Shakespeare, the actual writing of the text is believed to have been accomplished by other hands, and without the playwright's knowledge or authority. *A Shrew* can thus be recognised as evidence about theatrical production in Elizabethan times, when there was no effective copyright and plays could easily be 'pirated'; but it is not recognised as a play written by Shakespeare. An editor may believe (as does Ann Thompson, editor of the New Cambridge edition of *The Taming of the Shrew*, that *A Shrew's* complete Sly-framework probably indicates the existence of a similar theatrical structure in performed versions of Shakespeare's play; but no editor has yet thought it appropriate to amalgamate the two texts to the extent of incorporating as a whole the theatrical device preserved in an unauthorised, non-Shakespearean text.

The approach of theatrical practitioners has been quite different. In the case of *The Taming of the Shrew*, theatrical practice began many years ago to prefer the dramatic opportunities offered by the text of *A Shrew* to considerations of textual purity and authorial ascription. Initially this strategy of theatrical appropriation was quite at odds with the views of the literary–critical and scholarly establishment, which was in search of textual and authorial authenticity: for not only was the incompleteness, the insufficiency of Shakespeare's play acknowledged; in addition elements of a text generally regarded as inadequate and self-evidently un-Shakespearean were being incorporated to satisfy the requirements of theatrical practice.

The science of textual scholarship as applied to Shakespeare has seen considerable change in recent years, though not everyone would agree that the discipline has accomplished the revolution that some of its practitioners claim. Certainly contemporary scholarly editions now aim to acknowledge these plays as dramatic scripts as well as written texts, and to take into account a play's theatrical history when attempting to produce an authoritative text. Most scholarship remains nonetheless committed to discovering or inferring the author's orignal intentions, and to producing a text which a reincarnated Shakespeare would be able to recognise and approve. In the theatre, the presence of that forbidding and ghostly mythological creature, the absent author, does not always bear with quite the same gravity on the activities of those who work on and reproduce the plays in performance. Hence in the theatre history of *The Taming of the Shrew* we can witness a bold opportunism that can be regarded either as iconoclastic or as pioneering: the amalgamation of 'good' and 'bad' texts is taken to an extreme that more conservative scholars may disapprove, while their more progressive colleagues may look for ways of pursuing the theatre's natural dramatic instincts.

It is possible to attempt some distinctions between the two texts of the *Shrew* by looking at the evidence of their respective stage directions. The Folio text of *The Taming of the Shrew* certanly bears more traces of the Shakespearean 'hand' than does *The Taming of a Shrew*:[5] but while the latter is certainly an acting version, and may be some kind of transcript of an actual performance, it has been observed that the former, on account of inaccuracy and confusion in stage directions and speech headings, 'could not have been used in the theatre'.[6]

A radical divergence of staging between the two texts occurs at the end of the first scene. The opening of Shakespeare's second 'Induction' scene gives:

> *Enter aloft the drunkard with attendants, some with apparel, Bason and Ewer, and other appurtenances, and Lord*

The parallel stage direction in *The Taming of a Shrew* reads:

> *Enter two with a table and a banquet on it, and two other, with Slie asleepe in a chaire, richlie apparrelled, and the musick playing* (Praetorius, p. 6)

The Folio stage direction assumes that the rest of I.i. and the whole of I.ii. could have been played 'aloft': that is, we can with some confidence assume, in the gallery or balcony which overlooked the stage in a typical Elizabethan playhouse at the time of this play's original production. No other part of the play (and no part at all of *The Taming of a Shrew*) requires any space other than the bare platform stage available in all public theatres, and conjecturally in inn-yards and other non-purpose-built theatrical venues. Unless there are some hitherto undiscovered facts of Elizabethan stage history, this indicates that an important and elaborate episode would have been played in a confined space out of sight of some members of the audience: and in an excellent discussion Ann Thompson has shown that it is highly unlikely that this could conveniently have been done – too many actors are involved, there is too much detailed business with props, and the temporal extent of an episode sustained in the acting area 'aloft' is too long for normal Elizabethan stage practice. The Quarto stipulates that all the Sly-scenes take place on the main stage, which is much more ✗ probable: '. . . by far the major part of any play was enacted upon the projecting platform, with episode following episode in swift succession, and with shifts of time and place signalled to the audience only by the momentary clearing of the stage between episodes.'[7]

In addition, the Quarto stage direction specifies the number of actors to enter, where the Folio is vague ('with attendants'); props such as table, banquet and chair are listed (Folio's 'other appurtenances' is of little use to someone charged with the responsibilities of stage management: whereas the table brought on at this point in the Quarto evidently remains, and is used to considerable effect at a later point in the action), Sly's costume is defined, and the cue for atmospheric music supplied. This then is either a detailed description of what actually happened in performance, or a practicable set of directions to the actors. The stage direction in the Folio is, in short, not a stage direction proper but a bundle of hints and tentative suggestions from the author as to how the scene might be done: it has the imprecision and generality of the study rather than the practical imperatives of the tiring-room. The instruction for the actors to move 'aloft' was probably tried and rejected in rehearsal.

The stage directions in *A Shrew* display throughout a detailed, particularising quality by comparison with *The Shrew*: Shakespeare's '*Enter Petruchio and Grumio*' (III.ii.76) compares with the Quarto's '*Enter Ferando [Petruchio] baselie attired, and a red cap on his head*' (Praetorius, p. 22); '*Enter servants with supper*' (IV.i.113) reads in *A Shrew* as '*They cover the board and fetch in the*

[5]

meat . . . *He throws down the table and meat and all, and beats them*'
(Praetorius, p. 29). Whether we think of the Quarto as a script *for*
performance or a transcript *of* performance, it is clear that its
incidental instructions bring us closer to contemporary
Elizabethan theatrical practice than the vague suggestions of the
Folio.

I am not arguing that we can distinguish in any evaluative way
between a more strictly 'literary' mode of production traceable to
the cloistered creativity of the 'author', and a 'theatrical' mode
deriving from the rough practicalities of the playhouse. Since the
author in question was no poet hidden in the light of thought, but
a species of theatrical entrepreneur – actor, writer and speculative
businessman – his role in the process of production is likely to
have been a more consistent and sustained involvement than the
transmission of a completed text to a distinct group of actors. It
is now widely recognised by scholars that the discrete texts of a
Renaissance play represent a cultural activity in process, glimpsed
at different stages of a productive working in which the 'text' was
primarily regarded not as a finished commodity but as a script
for performance, remarkably alterable and subject to the conditions governing theatrical presentation at any given time. The
rudimentary stage directions of the Folio thus represent not naive
gesturings towards an absent performance, but specific proposals
to be attempted, improvised, modified or rejected by a collaborative team of theatrical practitioners at work. Such teams of practitioners have made an amalgamation of two texts a theatrical
norm: whereas textual scholars continue to reproduce the apparently incomplete Folio text. The modern descendants of those
Elizabethan actors have focused, not with the critics and scholars
on the internal organisation, formal coherence and imaginative
unity of individual texts; but on the lost but recoverable theatrical
practice still visible in the interstices of a text, eloquent in the
lacunae between one text and another, and implicit in the material
conditions of a theatre eternally restless to interrogate and reopen
the closures of written fiction, perpetually resistant to the notion
of a sealed and finished form.

Where much criticism and scholarship presupposes Philip
Edwards's dictum that 'the nearer we get to the stage, the further
we are getting from Shakespeare'[8]: this study is based on the alternative premise that 'Shakespeare' is no metaphysical subject of
individual authorship, but a collaborative medium of theatrical

presentation: 'Shakespeare' is not prior or superior to 'Shakespeare-in-performance'. The one is inextricably involved with the other, and both are components of a larger process: constituent elements in a perpetually contemporary cultural enterprise.

II Play and deception

The decision as to whether to include or exclude Christopher Sly is not a matter of an ordinary playhouse cut: without Christopher Sly the *Shrew* becomes a different play. As we shall see when examining the Zeffirelli film and Jonathan Miller's BBC/Time-Life-TV production, the excision of the Sly-frame converts the play into a naturalistic comedy (with varying degrees of farce) in which issues of marriage and sexual politics are dramatised (with more or less seriousness) by actors presenting themselves as real characters within a convincingly realistic social and domestic setting. Retention of the Sly-frame creates an entirely different dramatic medium: for the 'inner play' is designated by that frame as an elaborate hoax – part of a series of tricks calculated to fool a poor man into a temporary illusion of riches and power; a contrived fantasy designed (unsuccessfully, as it proves) to keep a drowsy itinerant awake. The 'Induction' of the Folio text alone establishes a theatrical perspective in which the action of the play is illuminated, by stimulating in the audience an invigorated sceptical consciousness, as an enacted artifice: while the entire Sly-frame confronts the audience with a continual, *unforgettable* reminder that the actors of the *Shrew* play are a fortuitously-gathered bunch of travelling players capriciously engaged to enact a whimsical nobleman's practical joke.

The 'Induction' plays with an entire vocabulary of illusion: 'practice', 'flatt'ring dream', 'worthless fancy', 'play', 'usurp' – a discourse which operates implicitly to link the delusion practised on Christopher Sly with the persuasive artifice of the drama itself. In comedy and tragedy illusion is both false and true, as what the theatre represents is both real and artificial. 'If this were played upon a stage now, I could condemn it as an improbable fiction' (*Twelfth Night*, III.iv.140-1). We assent to Fabian's remark: yet although the play is an improbable fiction, we don't for all that 'condemn' it. Viola's story of her sister in the same play (II.iv) is a mere tale improvised to extricate her from an awkward impasse; yet it expresses some deep and moving truth about herself. Othello's epic tales of heroic adventure induct his audience into the realms of fantasy: yet they are a true constitutive element both of his character and of his relationship with Desdemona. His suspicion of Desdemona is a colossal illusion: yet it has reality and power sufficient to shape for both of them a tragic destiny.

In history and farce, illusion has quite a different weight and value. In history it is an evasion or refusal of historical necessity, like the pastoral fantasies of Richard II or Henry VI. In farce it comes close to being mere deception, sharp practice, delusion. In farce the basic facts of life are crudely simple – lust, opportunism, con-artistry: so it is the more extraordinary and the more grotesquely comic that the hoodwinked subject – husband, dupe, fool – is unable to see what is so abundantly plain to the audience. In the *Shrew* plays, the romantic sub-plot derives, through Gascoigne and Ariosto, from Roman comedy, in which farce predominates over comedy, and illusions are 'counterfeit supposes' that cloud the judgement, blear the eye.

The *Shrew* plays were variously categorised as 'comedy' (in the Folio) or, in the words of the Quarto's title-page, 'a pleasant conceited history'. Shakespeare's play contains the tantalising self-definition of comedy as 'a kind of history', a *rapprochement* which invokes expectations of both fact and fiction. Whatever the complex interrelations between these two disparate forms, it can be suggested that the *Shrew* belongs more properly with those genres of 'history' and 'farce' which present illusion principally as deception, trickery or theatrical legerdemain.

The relationship proposed in the 'Induction' between 'illusion' and 'reality' is linked with analogous connections: wealth and poverty, impotence and power. Christopher Sly defines his own poverty in the very act of invoking, like Hardy's John Durbeyfield, a mythical charter of ancestral lineage: 'Look in the Chronicles . . . we came in with Richard Conqueror.' The authorising fantasy of noble descent has of course no effective power: whoever he came in with, he is thrown out as plain Christopher Sly of Burton-Heath. The Lord's decision to 'practice on this drunken man' leads to a transformation, by artifice, of the drunken tinker, rapt by fiction into self-oblivion, to an imaginary Lord: 'Would not the beggar then forget himself?' The category of fantasy is tied firmly, as in the Lord's phrase, 'flatt'ring dream', to relationships of authority and subordination: Sly is to be persuaded of the authenticity of his transformation by being offered 'submissive reverence' from ostensibly obsequious servants: 'Look how your servants do attend on you' – I am served, therefore I am whatever my servants tell me I am. The transformation of the page into a woman is identical to that of Sly, except that the page is in on the joke: and again the metamorphosis involves assumptions of authority – the page/woman is to serve Sly, 'do him obeisance' in a wish-fulfilment fantasy of female subordination, and thereby persuade Sly of the reality of his own transformation – 'I am your wife, in all obedience.'

'I am your wife, in all obedience'. The charm is wound up: the gulling of Christopher Sly complete. There is, however, a further dimension to the drama beyond this represented action, the deluding of a tinker: the relationship between what is happening within the stage-action, and the theatrical event itself; between the play and the play's own self-consciousness. The transformation of boy into woman was of course standard Elizabethan stage practice: but here the practice has its mechanisms exposed, its devices laid bare. The convention of cross-gender casting which must to an extent have naturalised the boy player within the female role is here subverted, so that the audience can acquire a self-conscious, metadramatic awareness of the illusion. In place of the usual spectacle of boy-actor-impersonating-woman, the Elizabethan spectators saw a boy player, acting the part of a page, directed by specific 'instructions' (Ind.I.126) to 'usurp the grace' (127) of the female sex. The page's maleness is considered to render him inexpert at the voluntary production of those artificial tears, designated by the Lord as peculiarly 'a woman's gift' (120), which might be required for the part. The inadequacy may be remedied, the tears supplied, by the application of an artificial stimulant:

> An onion will do well for such a shift,
> Which in a napkin being close conveyed
> Shall in despite enforce a watery eye. (Ind.I.122-4)

Like the references of the Chorus in *Henry V* to the 'four or five most vile and ragged foils' employed in productions of that play to signify the broadswords of Agincourt, such an allusion subverts conventional dramatic practices and properties which an audience would otherwise accept as perfectly adequate representations of reality.[9]

The super-objective of the page's dissimulation is the constitution of Sly, by an inversion of feudal categories, as an ersatz aristocrat – 'When they do *homage* to this simple *peasant*' (Ind.I.131). The group of players which is to perform a comedy within the play, and which thereby has some relationship of analogy with the Elizabethan acting company that performed *The Taming of the Shrew*, is also defined explicitly as a body of servants: 'players/ That offer service' (Ind.I.174) to the Lord: 'so please your Lordship to accept our duty' (78). Like the huntsmen who offer to

> ... play our part
> As he shall think by our true diligence
> He is no less than what we say he is ... (Ind.I.65-7)

when the players agree to perform, they contract not only voluntarily to offer a cultural service to an aristocratic patron, but to play a part assigned to them by that patron: their 'part' in the play is a 'part' in the plot to delude Christopher Sly, persuade him that he is 'no less than what [they] say he is' (67).

If the main action of the drama – *Catherine and Petruchio*, as Garrick entitled his Sly-free adaptation – is understood by the audience to be a model of theatrical performance in general, then it is entirely subversive of dramatic illusion and theatrical 'reality', since the 'play' is exposed as a 'flatt'ring dream or worthless fancy' (Ind.I.40), the 'sport' (87) or 'pastime' (63) of an idle nobleman. The players' craftsmanship and professional skills are viewed reductively in the illuminating term 'cunning' (88) which hovers curiously between the older sense of 'knowledge' and the newer meaning of crafty and calculating cleverness.[10] As the servants and players conspire to constitute Christopher Sly's reality – his expulsion at the hands of the hostess – as 'abject lowly dreams', the spectators of *The Taming of the Shrew* may begin to ask themselves if the play is not similarly suppressing and occluding their own reality and replacing it with a persuasive fantasy. The fantasies offered to Sly are all masculine wish-fulfilment dreams of pleasure and power: a luxurious couch equipped for the performance of lust; the aristocratic pleasures of hunting with horse, hawk and hound. The contents of the *Shrew* play are constantly being adumbrated in the 'Induction': in presenting Sly with a collection of paintings, the servants inflame his erotic fantasies and tempt his penchant for dreams of masculine domination, partly by playing with the dangerous equivocations of artistic realism:

[10]

> We'll show thee Io . . .
> As lively painted as the deed was done . . .
> Or Daphne . . .
> So workmanlike the blood and tears are drawn . . . (Ind.II.50-6)

These legends of subdued women, depicted with a wholly convincing appearance of reality, correspond directly to the *Shrew*-play itself, which similarly presents, by realistic *fabliau* techniques, a compelling myth of women subordinated to the reason and power of men.

The moment of Sly's submission to illusion, which in the epilogue to *A Shrew* is paralleled by a corresponding moment of awakening, has more than comic reverberations:

> Am I a lord, and have I such a lady?
> Or did I dream? Or have I dreamed till now?
> I do not sleep: I see, I hear, I speak,
> I smell sweet savours and I feel soft things . . .
> Upon my life, I am a lord indeed,
> And not a tinker, nor Christopher Sly. (64-9)

The pathos of these lines derives not only from the elements of guilt and shame that lacerate the pleasures of witnessing innocence beguiled: for the audience this is a moment of theatrical truth. The spectators watch a man wholly absorbed in illusion, entirely convinced by the tangible concreteness of his immediate sensations, that his life has been transformed. But what the spectator sees is similarly capable of being apprehended as an illusion, wherein actors impersonate utterly fictional characters, bring to life a wholly imaginary place and time, and endeavour with persuasive art to bestow truth on falsehood, convert illusion to reality, 'give to airy nothings / A local habitation and a name'. Is the spectator of *The Taming of the Shrew* as much a victim of illusion as the tinker? Is every playgoer an '*hypocrite lecteur*', the '*semblable et frère*' of Christopher Sly?

III   Production values

I want in this section to consider (in so far as it is possible) in a Renaissance historical context, those aspects of the play that have a bearing on stage design and on production 'style': geographical and historical setting, acting methods and costume.

The fact that compared with later conventions of stage-setting, specific geographical and historical locations in plays had relatively few 'stage design' implications for the Elizabethan theatres, is paradoxically a matter of some importance. Although the players in the purpose-built public playhouses could presumably have used illusionistic scenery and elaborate props to localise time and space, they evidently did not: in the style of the popular drama from which the Renaissance theatre evolved, they were content with rudimentary props and made no attempt at scenic illusion. The Eizabethan public theatre maintained some of the unlocalised qualities of the popular drama, a practice to which neo-classical critics like Sir Philip Sidney (in his *Defence of Poesie*, 1595) indignantly objected, in the belief that such dramatic liberty violated the fundamental laws of drama. For a stage without pictorial scenery or any other means of signifying place, location could be signified either verbally or via the language of costume. *The Taming of the Shrew* is set in Padua, *The Taming of a Shrew* in Athens: but when these two plays (if they were two plays) were performed in the Renaissance public playhouse, the stage retained an identical visual appearance: each drama was enacted on that same physical space of bare thrust stage, plain or curtained tiring-house facade, two doors and a gallery above.

Although Renaissance plays are often highly specific in their constructions of the past and of other societies,[11] the representation of place on their stages was thus entirely unlocalised. This does not indicate that 'Athens' and 'Padua' were quite meaningless or relativistic terms: on the contrary, the discourses of classicising romance and of Italianate commercialism so prominent respectively in *A Shrew* and *The Shrew* are thereby located in appropriate historico-geographical contexts. What it does indicate is that the stage could represent 'both many days, and many places' without any recourse to the mechanical construction of scenic illusion. In *The Taming of the Shrew*, the location of the primary dramatic narrative shifts from a rural and provincial English location, linked by place-names to Shakespeare's native Warwickshire, to the Italian commercial and academic city of Padua; but on the Elizabethan stage this shift probably involved nothing of what we consider to be a 'scene-change'.

The material conditions of a play's historical origin, the physical architecture and shape of the originating performance space, exercised a determining influence on its dramatic structure and theatrical rhythm. Since space and time were not represented visually, they remained flexible and relative dimensions of dramatic narrative, which could be realised as objectively present, or estranged into fictional distance, by the verbal and gestic codes of the drama. Just as the Christopher Sly 'Induction' introduces into the play a fundamental indeterminacy about the relations of reality and illusion so the unlocalised theatrical practice of the Elizabethan public stage constructed within these dramatic narratives an indeterminate relationship between present and past, the exotic and the immediate, here and now and there and then. The implications of these facts for modern theatrical practice are profound: since they indicate that, in so far as productions are incorporated into nineteenth-century traditions of pictorial realism and illusionistic staging, they will operate to fix time and place in a manner entirely foreign to the indeterminacy and flexibility of the Renaissance theatre. Discussion of the consequences of that introduced constraint necessarily involves value-judgements which are better canvassed in relation to specific productions than theoretically; and since the two most widely-seen and influential productions discussed here – a film and a television version – operate within the nineteenth-century conventions of pictorial realism, some sharp distinctions and discriminations will have to be made.

The other principal ingredient of Elizabethan stagecraft, acting method, is again difficult to discuss: since there is little surviving concrete information and in the space of that absent evidence flourishes a plenitude of myths. Hamlet's advice to the travelling players who arrive in Elsinore as opportunely as their counterparts turn up in *The Shrew* has been accepted almost universally[12] as a record of Shakespeare's personal observations on principles of acting. Yet an adherence to the kinds of naturalism and neo-classical decorum there advocated would render the role of Hamlet (which involves assuming the melodramatic rant of the revenge hero) unplayable; and that play itself could scarcely be contained, as Sidney's critique would suggest, within the Aristotelian principles of the Prince's expressed dramatic theory.[13]

There is little doubt that during the period of Shakespeare's professional career the drama became more realistic: though it is highly questionable, and to me extremely improbable, that any kind of naturalism was ever a dominant method. The internal evidence of the plays points rather to a considerable range and variety of acting methods, consistent with certain constitutive features of the Elizabethan theatre: the flexibility of the unlocalised acting area; the heterogeneity of its theatrical influences and antecedents; and the generic variety of the dramatic medium. A theatrical space without specific location does not call for any particular style of acting, by contrast with an illusionistic set which requires naturalism of speech and behaviour: if space and time are relative and iterable, so is the vehicle by means of which actors occupy that imaginative dimension. Acting can be naturalistic, expressionistic, emblematic, metadramatic, alienatory at different points in a single play.

There is, again, hardly enough external evidence about the uses of costume on the early Elizabethan stage to form the basis for a serious historical discussion: we only know that plays were performed in some combination of contemporary dress, historical costume, and gestural probably emblematic signs of cultural context. It is necessary, in the absence of more contextual evidence, to examine the internal details of the play-texts for information about costume: and certainly in *The Taming of the Shrew* we soon discover that costume is one of the principal theatrical languages of the stage narrative. The language of clothes begins to speak with Christopher Sly:

> Ne'er ask me what raiment I'll wear, for I have no more doublets than backs, no more stockings than legs, nor no more shoes than feet – nay, sometimes more feet than shoes, or such shoes as my toes look through the overleather. (Ind.II.7-10)

This sartorial self-portrait is so specific in its depiction of Elizabethan costume – doublets, stockings – that it will raise problems for a naturalistic 'modern-dress' production, or for one set in any other period. Furthermore it is a description of a condition of poverty and deprivation signified by dress, which a stage production will have to express in one way or another, and which would presumably have been directly represented on the Elizabethan stage. The very notion of transformation, if it is to be visually enacted, depends on clear and sharp distinctions between one costume and another: and for the audience immediate recognition of the meanings attached to particular styles of dress.

In the case of the tinker's metamorphosis the passage from poverty to affluence presents no difficulty; but the next transformation encountered in the play is far less clear-cut for a modern audience than it would have been for the Elizabethans –

> *Lucentio*: Tranio, at once
> Uncase thee; take my coloured hat and cloak. (I.i.197-8)

The exchange of outer garments would be quite meaningless to an audience unless the two characters were immediately recognisable by the codes of their dress as fashionable master and liveried servant. As a process of exchanging meaning, transformation by dress discloses a deeply interesting relationship between ideology and theatrical art. The meanings expressed by clothes in Tudor society were not regarded as arbitrary socially-constructed distinctions of function, but as inherent differences of rank, natural, even biological in origin. Yet these meanings were invested in signs external to the body, easy to remove or change. The theatre specialised in the inversion, substitution and transgression of these sartorial codes, which bore some of society's fundamental political meanings: this is doubtless one of the many reasons why an institution which has often been evaluated in historical criticism as an ideological state apparatus was frequently suspected in its own time of subversive and seditious influence. Counter to the ideological assumption that distinctions of rank were natural, the play seems to draw attention to fashion's arbitrary system of signs, to the biological similarity of people across divisions of family, kin and class:

> Nor can we be distinguished by our faces
> For man or master. (I.i.191-2)

In the play's medium of comic transformation a mere switch of clothes alters distinctions traditionally held immutable. The language of clothes is clearly recognised here as an eloquent but unstable discursive system.

Further inversion of the visual codes of fashion occurs at the wedding of Katherina and Petruchio, where the bridegroom denies the expectation of conventional nuptial apparel, and is described as an apparition of the grotesque:

> Petruchio is coming in a new hat and old jerkin; a pair of old breeches thrice turned; a pair of boots that have been candle-cases, one buckled, another laced; an old rusty sword tane out of the town armoury, with a broken hilt and chapless; with two broken points . . . his lackey . . . with a linen stock on one leg and a kersey boot-hose on the other,

> gartered with a red and blue list; an old hat and the humour of forty
> fancies pricked in't for a feather; a monster, a very monster in
> apparel, and not like a Christian footboy or a gentleman's lackey.

The bravura rhetoric of this reported description excites in an audience expectations which the stagecraft of the production must endeavour to fulfil: Petruchio and Grumio must look at least as ludicrous as Biondello's farcical portrayal, and the distance in visual impression between a 'gentleman's lackey' and a 'monster in apparel' must be clearly and unmistakably demarcated.

Baptista explicitly endorses the conventional relationship between clothes and social meanings, criticising Petruchio's 'unreverent robes' as a 'shame to (his) estate' and 'an eye-sore to our solemn festival'. Petruchio denies that there is any such stable relationship between clothes and the wearer: the relationship he claims between himself and Kate is much more direct, body to body, dispensing with the signifying systems of dress – 'To me she's married, not unto my clothes.' The visual grotesque of Petruchio's stipulated costume is a necessary context for this puritanical affirmation of unclothed morality, which in turn enters into contradiction with Petruchio's very obvious use of his own eccentric but nonetheless authoritarian signifying code. Petruchio imposes the same ethic of counter-fashion on Kate herself in the 'tailor-scene' (IV.iii.3) which decisively foregrounds the play's self-conscious interrogation of the language of dress. Petruchio's denunciation of the fashionable Italian cap and elaborate designer gown supplied for his wife, incorporating as it does the details of a dressmaker's inventory, could hardly be more specific as instructions to a costume designer, and faces the modern producer with clear-cut choices: between adherence to Renaissance costume, the cutting or rewriting of the lines, or the adoption of a non-naturalistic technique which refuses any direct relationship between verbal and visual languages. The comic energy of the scene contains a curious ambivalence between the avowed puritan distaste for extravagances of dress, and an obsessively literal preoccupation with the physical appearance and texture of clothes. When at the end of the play Petruchio wishes to demonstrate Kate's spontaneous obedience, he does so via this pervasive language of costume: 'Doff thy cap . . .'. 'Costume' is not by any means an optional addition to the substantive meaning of a Renaissance play: together with other constituent dialects of the language of performance, it is a primary signifier, an indespensible bearer of theatrical meaning.

All histories of Renaissance drama in interpretation or production may be said to reside between two polarised positions. At one extreme lies the traditional historicist and literary–critical assumption that a play is a stable, immanent, 'authored' entity, which in turn authorises and polices the boundaries of its own system of reproduction; at the other lies the theatrical or 'deconstructionist' premise that a play exists only in its productions, as a book exists only in its readings. The former position would deduce from the above discussion that *The Taming of the Shrew* would be performed, as most of the productions discussed here were performed, in 'traditional' costume: that is, the reconstructed Renaissance costume which began to appear on the stage in the course of the nineteenth century. The latter position would infer that the originating moment of a text's production exercises no control over its subsequent reproduction in criticism and performance: that the text is raw material for the construction of contemporary meaning. Both traditional literary criticism and a powerful body of opinion within dramatic criticism, associated particularly with the name of John Barton,[14] would argue that a body of 'intentions' or 'directions' inscribed into the text by its author can be elicited from it in the practices of textual criticism and theatrical experiment; while many theatrical practitioners would insist, together with deconstructionist critics, on the necessary independence and autonomy of their creative efforts. It seems to me that an exploration of the internalised language of costume demonstrates that a distinct level of meaning *is* inscribed within and *can* be disclosed from, the text; but that it would be mere conformism and abject submission to the power of bardolatry to regard that inscription as prescriptive rather than indicative, as historically determining rather than historically determined. Theoretically then, decisions about stage and costume design and acting methods in any given production are essentially voluntary; provided only that the production recognises the extent to which within the text meaning is habitually encoded in a language of space, dress and mimetic art.

IV Multiple plots

If the Christopher Sly framework is incorporated, the *Shrew* becomes a play with three separable centres of action, or three interwoven plots: the gulling of Christopher Sly, the wooing/taming of Katherina by Petruchio, and the courtship romance built around the figure of Bianca. The relationship between the Katherina and Bianca narratives is hardly an instance of densely-woven organic interdependence, like *Henry IV* or *Twelfth Night*: which may be one reason why the Bianca plot has frequently been squeezed virtually into a marginal episode, as in Zeffirelli's film; or occluded altogether, as in Garrick's version. Although its presence could hardly subvert the dominant centrality of the Katherina–Petruchio narrative, it does make available a number of important emphases, and without it the play becomes something quite different.

The Bianca-plot allows for a sustained contrast between the characters and actions of the two sisters, which becomes at certain points (especially with the rather arbitrary introduction of Hortensio's widow) a deployment and interplaying of different modes of feminine behaviour. In more naturalistic productions like Jonathan Miller's, much can be made of the manifest and violent sibling rivalry between the two sisters; while more feministic productions like Michael Bogdanov's need the presence of other women, either to indicate that Katherina's history is no isolated eccentricity but a general condition; or as a means of establishing and evaluating female reactions to Katherina's 'shrewishness' and to her 'taming'. The courtship narrative that features Bianca, although humorously treated, serves as a more conventional model of romance fiction to throw the bizarre and unorthodox wooing of Petruchio into sharp and dislocating relief: in Zeffirelli's film what little remains of Bianca and her suitors is used principally to clarify and validate the boisterous anti-romance of Petruchio's assault on conventional Paduan values.

But the most important function of the Bianca plot within the play as a whole lies in its emphasis on disguise and illusion: a thematic strategy which operates both at the narrative level of romance and comic courtship disguises, and at the psychological level of complicating an audience's perspective on Bianca – does she prove, many commentators have asked, the verier shrew of

[18]

the two? – and on Katherina and Petruchio – are they truly what they seem? The thematic context of pretence, dissimulation, illusion, broached by the Christopher Sly framework, is thus played with at various different levels: the travelling players assume the disguises of Bianca, Katherina and Petruchio, whose roles may themselves mask 'true identity' behind a facade of deceptive conformity or outrageously unconventional behaviour. Modern actors assume the roles of Elizabethan actors who assume roles like Lucentio and Hortensio, which then require further levels of duplicitous disguising as they assume the identities of Cambio and Licio. A focus on the Bianca plot can thus disclose in the *Shrew* a dramatic structure of some intricacy: not in terms of delicately interwoven tissues of metaphor, or of elaborate pychological counterpointing of character; but in terms of a vertiginously Pirandellian interaction of theatrical illusion and dramatic 'reality'. John Barton's 1960 production marks the beginning of a series of such metadramatic theatrically self-conscious *Shrews*.

This multiplicity of plot involves also, considering the varied natures of the three centres of action, a striking degree of generic heterogeneity. The *Shrew* derives its dramatic material from a wide variety of generic sources – folk-tale, romance, satire, the medieval literature of misogyny and the traditions of Roman comedy. The Sly induction takes place in Warwickshire, the play of Katherina and Petruchio in Padua; both Sly and Petruchio owe much to very ancient fables and legends, while Bianca is a product of medieval romance and Roman comedy.

This diversity of generic content has implications for all the components of performance. Can a play of such internal complexity be contained within one dramatic style? Is it possible to reduce such a theatrical text to a single set and a uniform style of playing? Which is the obvious departure point for the imaginations of set- and costume-designers – the Warwickshire inn of Christopher Sly's ejection, the Renaissance Padua of Baptista and Bianca, the bizarre Gothic fantasy of Petruchio's house?

Different directors, as we shall see, have responded to these problems in very dfferent ways. One feature that is common to all the productions here discussed is that this generic discontinuity insistently demands inconsistency in methods and styles of acting. The text of *The Taming of the Shrew*, with its dizzying shifts from sentimental romance to vigorous satire, from grotesque and uninhibited farce to puritanical earnestness, from sensitive psychological insight to the crudest brutality, calls for considerable flexibility and range from its performers, and for the most open and unlocalised acting space. The drama of the public playhouses evolved from a variety of sources, in both popular and educated drama, which must in turn have involved very different acting styles, from the most academic historical realism to the most self-conscious and fictive art of comedy. In *The Taming of a Shrew*, there are continual abrupt and dislocating shifts between a classicising romanticism reminiscent of Marlowe, and a crude saturnalian horseplay derived from popular forms of enterainment. *The Taming of the Shrew*, is, in other words, a typical example of the 'impure' art of the Renaissance theatre which proved so offensive to the principles of neo-classical critical theory. More literary forms of criticism, in paradoxical conflict with their neoclassical antecedents, have sought to emphasise the formal craftsmanship and aesthetic skill with which these heterogeneous elements were reduced to a single unified action. But *dramatic* criticism, drawing on the evidence of theatrical practice, should bestow more attention on the rich plurality of such a diversified theatrical medium. Stanley Wells, reviewing Jonathan Miller's BBC *Shrew*, objected to the eclectic inconsistency of acting methods employed:

> As Tranio, Anthony Pedley deployed the full armoury of the farce actor, with exaggerated facial expressions and grotesque speech characteristics – dropped and misplaced aspirates, impure vowels, glottal stops, affectations of gentility. If all around him had been playing in the same mode, we might have admired; as they were not, we remained unconvinced.[15]

The ghost of Sir Philip Sidney is raised by these observations; not to mention the curious echoes of Rudyard Kipling ('If all around him') and Queen Victoria ('we remained unconvinced'). But the post-Wagnerian quest for unity of style can gain little purchase on a product of the Renaissance public playhouse. If all the actors had been 'playing in the same mode', it is difficult to imagine how they could have been performing *The Taming of the Shrew*.

V   Sexual politics

Much contemporary interest in the play derives from the development of feminist criticism and theory, and rests in its very direct and controversial address to issues of gender politics. There is no space here to review the various arguments from feminist criticism,[16] and specific account will be taken of the sexual ideology of each production discussed. I want to look here at the play's relationship with its historico-cultural context, and at historiographical attempts to reconstruct those social practices and institutions which inscribed within the play its potentialities for releasing gender-political discourse.

A quite specific historical context for the *The Taming of the Shrew* can be assembled from the social historiography of Christopher Hill, Lawrence Stone and other writers on this period. The principal emphasis of these historians of domestic culture is on large-scale and far-reaching changes in the institution of marriage during the Tudor period, changes accelerated and consolidated by the rise of Puritanism and the Revolution. Christopher Hill speaks of a 'sexual revolution' which eventually replaced property marriage by 'a monogamous partnership in the affairs of the family';[17] and Lawrence Stone has argued for the view that in this period an older dynastic and familial concept of marriage as a property and kinship relationship was beginning to give way to 'companionate marriage' and to the 'nuclear family'.[18] Though few would seriously argue that the period saw widespread female emancipation (and Stone believes that Puritan marriages actually enhanced rather than diminished patriarchal power) it is evident that there was, as Catherine Belsey puts it, 'a contest for the meaning of the family in the sixteenth and seventeenth centuries which unfixed the existing system of differences'.[19] Such 'unfixing' of traditional stereotypes and social roles is naturally of interest to feminism: and Juliet Dusinberre in her study *Shakespeare and the Nature of Women* emphasises the Puritan revaluation of marriage – 'replacing the legal union of the arranged marriage with a union born of the spirit'[20] – as a significant factor in the development of female independence.

It is tempting to see these historical changes reflected explicitly in the play: and Jonathan Miller's BBC production seems to have been intended as an illustration of just such a cultural change in the institution of marriage, informed by the spirit of Puritanism. Petruchio's contempt for traditional social forms, his insistence on marriage as a direct and exclusive relationship between himself and Katherina, his immediate withdrawal of his wife from her kin to his own house, can all be seen as expressive of the newer concep-

[21]

tion of marriage. In addition Petruchio constantly voices sentiments easy to associate with Puritanism – 'To me she's married, not unto my clothes'; ''Tis the mind that makes the body rich' – and in Miller's view the taming-process itself symbolises a relationship of genuine mutuality, with Petruchio redeeming Katherina, for their mutual benefit, from the curse of her shrewish nature.

Unfortunately this interpretation is not an adequate historicist account of the play. A principal emphasis of the new conception of marriage was the importance of free choice for the partners, as against the old system of parental arrangement: the voluntary emotional contract of a couple becoming more important than the legal and financial contract engaged in by the parents. But Petruchio acquires Kate by a commercial agreement with her father, without even inspecting his acquisition first: and at no point is she given the opportunity to express her inclination. The 'taming-plot' allows for no such expression of female independence: it is the romantic sub-plot that gives the younger sister Bianca her free choice of partner. Petruchio's is no companionate Puritan marriage, but an old-fashioned commercial contract, representative of the very system Puritan marriage sought to replace. The taming-plot itself is, as we have seen, a narrative structure of great antiquity, a folklore form which embodies some of the most barbaric and oppressive attitudes towards women: the ideology it contains is quite different from the Puritan version of patriarchy, which emphasised reciprocal obligation and mutual respect, and which had to recognise – as Charles I discovered to his cost – the possibility of a false fatherhood from which it was legitimate to withold consent. Katherina's final speech of submission expresses an orthodox vision of social hierarchy and state power: in which the subordination of subject to prince, child to parent, wife to husband and citizen to magistrate, was a fundamental principle of civic order. Yet the logical end of Puritanism was a radical questioning of state authority, which in turn created the further possibility of questioning patriarchy: in 1641 the Leveller Mrs Chidley argued that just as a magistrate had no right to control a man's conscience, so in turn that man had no right to control his own wife's.

Given the specific historical context, it seems to me impossible, despite the sustained efforts of a huge critical and theatrical project of naturalising and domestication, to elicit from the given text of the *Shrew* a body of meanings and values compatible with modern progressive thought or with contemporary feminism. At the same time it seems equally unsatisfactory to regard the play as a 'barbaric and disgusting' relic of medieval misogyny. We have become accustomed to accepting that Shakespeare's plays, despite their evident complexity and apparent intellectual independence, may still be shown ultimately to speak for the dominant ideologies of state power and patriarchal authority. But we would hardly expect to find, given the general ideological cast of the plays, the kind of crude assertion of patriarchy which seems more calculated to call ideology into question than to naturalise it into acceptance. Furthermore, criticism has become perhaps too exclusively concerned to identify the political and cultural powers Renaissance theatre can be conjectured to have spoken *for*: at the price of neglecting the fundamental truth that all art – particularly the art of the Renaissance theatre – is a dialogue between producers and audience, and that these plays spoke *to* that audience as well as *for* certain powerful vested interests in society. A fundamentally anti-democratic bias characterised the historicist criticism of the Tillyard school, and has by no means been expunged from newer kinds of historical criticism: we have to be very wary of the assumption that quoting the letter of state propaganda or the dominant aesthetic language is an adequate way of describing the cultural life of a people. Arguments from demography and reception theory are of course notoriously more difficult to construct than arguments from centralised authority and cultural power. The agents of patriarchal authority in church and state recorded their views on the nature of marriage and the necessary subordination of women: while most of Shakespeare's audience went to their graves in silence.

It remains nonetheless possible to attempt some speculations about probable contemporary reactions to a play like *The Taming of the Shrew*. As a rule Renaissance plays express a positive appreciation of free choice, companionate relationship and romantic individualism in marriage, as opposed to parental authority, domestic inequality and impersonal contract. The audiences were metropolitan, more likely to be attuned to the more modern currents of contemporary thought: it was certainly illegal in London to batter a wife or even to call a woman a whore. We know that the Elizabethan audiences consisted of more than one social class, so that the variations in attitude towards marriage, noted by historians, between one social group and another, would probably be reflected. Lastly, the audiences contained women as well as men; and the two genders could be differentiated and addressed by the actors as separate constituencies within the unified audience (as in the epilogue to *As You Like It*) capable of differences of opinion and response.

It seems highly improbable that the blunt assertion of patriarchal power in the *Shrew* could have successfully imposed an ideological uniformity on such an audience, confirming the men in the security of their power, requiring dutiful submission from the women. The very sharpness of its sexual politics would seem to make the play provocative and polemical rather than persuasive: offering different kinds of challenge to both genders in the audience.

Further confirmation of this argument can be sought in an intertextual comparison with other versions of the play. Restoration and eighteenth-century adaptations were acutely sensitive to the problematical quality of its sexual politics, and modified the text accordingly: either for example by omitting the whole of the wife's final speech, or by giving the husband formal expressions of mutual love and reciprocal obligation. The most interesting case is the 1735 'ballad farce' *A Cure for a Scold*, which has an epilogue in which the actress gratefuly drops and distances herself firmly from her role as a wife:[21]

> Well, I must own it wounds me to the heart
> To act, unwomanly – so mean a part.

Of course it is self-evident that an adaptation made some two centuries later would inevitably reflect different attitudes to women! But it seems to me arguable that what is formally decoded in *A Cure for a Scold* was already encoded in Shakespeare's text: invisible, certainly, to a purely textual analysis, since its effects of alienation were inscribed within the perfomance medium of that particular kind of theatre, and in the dialectical relationships between actors and audience.

A more conclusive illustration is to be found in the completeness of the Christopher Sly framework in *The Taming of a Shrew*, If Sly was to be retained on stage throughout, the dramatic structure constituted by this provision of an onstage audience alters the nature of the theatrical event. If the play is in one sense a delusion practised on Christopher Sly, then it may be recognised as a delusion practised on the audience as well. When Sly at the end of *The Taming of a Shrew* proposes to go off and tame his wife, the crudity of the taming-plot is clearly acknowledged and exposed to the knowledge of the audience. I agree with Ann Thompson (New Cambridge Shakespeare) that despite the evidence of the Folio text Shakespeare's *Shrew* probably had in performance a complete Sly-framework (Thompson, *ed. cit.*, appendix 1). If it did, then it could have been performed in the self-reflexive, metadramatic and ironic manner of Brecht's epic theatre. Katherina's final speech of submission, which is in most stage productions explained as a private joke or intimate understanding between Katherina and Petruchio, might well have been delivered on the Elizabethan stage with appropriate detachment, distancing and irony to an audience highly sceptical of such propagandist rhetoric; offered as a challenge and provocation to debate rather than as an attempt at ideological incorporation.

The play itself, in its given textual form, cannot provide us with a definition of its own sexual politics. The pluralistic meanings that can be provoked by the text lie outside it, in the contradictory evidence of social history, and in the dialectic of theatrical performance.

CHAPTER II

John Barton (1960)

I

John Barton's 1960 production of *The Taming of the Shrew* dates from the first effective year of Peter Hall's directorship of the Shakespeare Memorial Theatre: the year we have come to regard as the *annus mirabilis* in which a provincial drama festival underwent a revolutionary transformation into the Royal Shakespeare Company. After the first performance of *The Shrew* the London *Evening Standard* carried a brief anecdote, under the by-line 'Sausages on the Lawn', which amusingly recreates some of the cultural tensions *apparently* involved in the whole RSC enterprise:

> At opposite ends of Stratford-on-Avon two parties flourished at opposite ends of the formality scale.
>
> Sir Fordham and Lady Flower entertained guests at their home, The Hill, to an elegant buffet supper that looked like a full-colour picture from a magazine devoted to gracious living.
>
> Director Peter Hall provided guests at his home, Avoncliffe, with sausages toasted on the lawn and jazz from a tape-recorder.
>
> Both parties celebrated the first night of *The Taming of the Shrew*, at the Shakespeare Memorial Theatre.
>
> Encouraged by this community of interest, some guests contrived to visit both soirées.
>
> Mr Hall arrived at The Hill without his wife, actress Leslie Caron. 'She's in Marseilles, making money', he said.[1]

As we look back at this detail through the accumulated noughts of Sir Peter Hall's income, the proposed set of oppositions – between patrician largesse and low-budget bohemianism, an aristocratic soirée and an avant-garde barbecue – start to form a rather different configuration; and we might well be more struck by the telling phrase 'community of interest' than by the modish radicalism attributed to Peter Hall's toasted sausages.

Although there is a danger of distorting in a retrospective survey the actual structure of an historical moment, this model of reconciliation between old and new Stratfords now seems an appropriate symbol of the RSC. The progressive ensemble company of the 1960s, with its radical credentials and experimental style, its contemporary political preoccupations and its resemblances to the Moscow Arts Theatre and the Berliner Ensemble, actually owed as much to the philanthropic ethos of a cultivated bourgeoisie as it did to the *petit-bourgeois* radicalism and entrepreneurial vision of Peter Hall. The wealthy Stratford brewing family which endowed the Shakespeare Memorial Theatre in 1877 was not by any means the philistine dynasty pilloried by the nineteenth-century London press. The original vision of Charles Flower, who initiated the chain of activities whch led eventually to the formation of the RSC (and who was also the first, incidentally, to occupy that residential tribute to gracious living, The Hill) was of a privately-subsidised permanent ensemble company modelled on the Meiningen company, whose work he evidently knew about, though they did not actually visit England until 1888. With his emphases on the centrality of the actor, on training, on the ensemble principle, and on the independence from commercial pressures guaranteed by patronage and subsidy, he seemed to be pointing the way towards the RSC rather than towards the Shakespeare Memorial Theatre of the mid-twentieth century.[2] And when the transition from the essentially occasional, artistically erratic and star-studded Stratford summer festivals of Anthony Quayle, Sir Barry Jackson and Glen Byam Shaw to Peter Hall's modern ensemble company did occur, it could not have done so without the support of Fordham Flower (Beauman, pp. 234-5). At the same time, subsequent developments in the commercial and political history of the RSC, and obviously in the career of (Sir) Peter Hall, should provoke us to ponder on whether the new-style RSC was a genuine cultural and political *alternative* to the dominant theatrical establishment: or rather one of the 'paradoxical means by which a dominant order ensures its own continuance'.[3] The current

Artistic Director of the RSC, Terry Hands, describes the organisation in very different terms from the controlling conception of Charles Flower, or the shaping vision of Peter Hall: 'Only one-third of our income comes from the government, not as a subsidy but as an investment. We are more akin to a merchant bank or an underwriting firm; we are maverick, buccaneer, private'.[4]

The transformation of the Shakespeare Memorial Theatre in 1960 has been thoroughly documented: those changes which are especially relevant to a discussion of Barton's *Shrew* were the formation of a permanent company; the re-designing of the Stratford stage; and a new emphasis on the training of actors, with special reference to the 'craft' of speaking Shakespearean verse.[5]

The permanent company was to be achieved by a new system of long-term contracts: though from the outset these were not strenuously binding on the artist – they included, for example, a 'suspension' clause whereby the actor could be temporarily free to work elsewhere (Addenbrooke, p. 268). It is evident that Peter Hall wanted the arrangement to be fairly open and flexible, so as to avoid discouraging those actors who could earn much higher salaries in, for example, the film industry: Hall wanted '. . . a fairly loose nucleus of actors who regarded this company as their permanent home, although they might go away from time to time in order to benefit from working in films and television'.[6] This may be seen as a sensible diplomatic proviso; but it did nothing to prevent the drift of successful actors away from the company, rendered the effective implementation of the ensemble principle very difficult, and arguably succeeded in retaining the services only of those actors who would have sustained a commitment to an artistically growing RSC in any event. Both Peter O'Toole and Peggy Ashcroft, the Petruchio and Katherina of John Barton's production of *The Shrew*, were among the first contract artists to be signed up. O'Toole was, he told journalists in 1960, 'wildly enthusiastic' about the contracts, and felt that 'this was the way actors ought to work'. He played, however, only the one season at Stratford; though Hall cast him in the role of Henry II in his own production of *Becket* for the following year, O'Toole promptly left the RSC to make *Lawrence of Arabia*. O'Toole's departure from Peter Hall's contract was thus no different from the earlier defection of his friend Richard Burton from Anthony Quayle's Shakespeare Memorial Theatre to Hollywood.

As the existence of long-term contracts was not announced until

[28]

October 1960, audience and critical reception of Barton's *Shrew* were not in any way affected by this particular change. The refashioning of the Shakespeare Memorial stage was a more obvious innovation, and was particularly noted as a striking feature of stage design. David Addenbrooke summarised the alterations:

> Three Renaissance arches, forming a false proscenium, were introduced to form a permanent setting for the season. The actual stage was re-shaped further out over the orchestra pit, and this extension incorporated a hand-operated revolve which spanned the width of the proscenium opening. The stage was raked, and the apron was cut away at both sides to allow two rows of angled seats to be added at the front of the stalls. The new stage apron extended 14 feet into the auditorium and was intended to bring the players into closer contact with the audience than had ever before been possible at Stratford. Hall declared that he wished to use the stage as a 'platform for the imagination': 'A stage would be very frankly a stage – not just an illusionist's bag of tricks'. (Addenbrooke, p. 44)

This redesigning of the stage was intended to accommodate a new emphasis on the centrality of the actor: 'a style in which visual effects would remain secondary to the speaking actor'.[7]

This preoccupation with verbal language derived, as Christopher J. McCullough has shown (*The Shakespeare Myth*, 1988, pp. 111-12), from a common inheritance of Cambridge English studies, shared by both Barton and Hall. It was more therefore than simply a concern with verbal communication: it was rather a new interest in *textuality*, in the written medium as the true vehicle of dramatic meaning. Addressing his actors, Hall advised them to reject Stanislavskian method, and to concentrate on textual rather than psychological understanding:

> An intelligent understanding of the form and expression of the text is as much the raw material of your creation as knowing the name of the character you are playing. We want to tell you about ends of lines, about rhyme, about the form of the verse, the nature of the verse, and verse speaking as a craft. We want you to think about these things in rehearsal in creative terms.[8]

It is in the light of this latter preoccupation that the otherwise somewhat unlikely appointment as Assistant Director of the Shakespeare Memorial Theatre of John Barton, Lay Dean of King's College, Cambridge, whose academic research interests were in the Elizabethan theatre and in the translation of Anglo-Saxon poetry, needs to be seen. In fact Barton was the product of a vigorous theatrical culture in post-war Cambridge, and his role in organisations such as the Marlowe Society indicates the relevance of his own confessed preference for the theatrical over the academic life. Barton nonetheless brought to the RSC certain essentially academic preoccupations with the nature of dramatic language, which left their distinct imprint on his work for the company and on the general character of the company itself.[9]

II

It was, in part, the director's academic and scholarly background – in addition to the already-existing Stratford tradition discussed in Chapter I – that evolved for this production an amalgamation of *The Taming of a Shrew* with the Shakespearean play. The augmentations were punctiliously pointed out in the programme notes, and thence brought to the attention of reviewers and spectators. The prompt-book shows a text of Shakespeare's play, re-divided into fourteen scenes, with additional typed passages from *A Shrew* pasted in.[10] Barton thus chose to employ the complete Sly-frame, and to foreground the metadramatic character of the play-within-a-play format, with the *Shrew* action presented by strolling players to an on-stage surrogate audience of Sly and his attendants. When the travelling players entered to the Lord, they appeared pushing their cart and carrying bundles; they engaged with the Lord in professional negotiations about the projected performance and required properties; and they included among their number a prompter, whose constant attempts to follow his script functioned to promote both comedy and a metadramatic awareness. This insistent foregrounding of the players as actors was sustained throughout the production: the permanent revolving set incorporated along with interior and exterior locations an inner 'green-room', in which the actors could be seen rehearsing, changing costumes, drinking and playing cards.

Furthermore, Barton developed the function of Sly as a foregrounded spectator. Sly observed the play from various points of vantage on the set, a bench, a gallery, a staircase (see illustration 1). As the set revolved he and the Lord (masquerading as the servant 'Sim' from *The Taming of a Shrew*) were obliged to scramble over a staircase to keep tabs on the action. The prompt-book contains cues for Sly's reactions to the events played out before him: thus the Lord's reference to 'my trusty servant, well-approved in all' is accompanied by a stage direction '*Sly applauds*'; and Lucentio's announcement that he intends to pursue 'a course of learning and ingenuous studies' receives the response '*Sly reacts with distaste*'. The performers of the play-within-the-play were directed to display awareness of Sly as spectator – thus stage directions such as '*actors bow to Sly*' appear frequently; and on occasions Sly could even make contact with the actors – '*Sly stops Grumio, who turns to him*'. As Vincentio was about to be unjustly imprisoned, Sly ran on to the set and stopped the action completely: 'Come, we'll have no sending to prison, that's flat.' The actors stumbled, lost their cues and had to be started off again by the offices of the prompter.

Critical reactions from reviewers uniformly gave attention to this aspect of the production, but varied considerably in their assessement of its success. The most negative response came from Bernard Levin, who saw Barton's handling of the play as the unpardonable imposition of scholarly theory on the sanctity of the Shakespearean text: a violation which ought to have been entitled 'The murder of Shakespeare in five acts':

> The trouble is that Shakespeare, after establishing Christopher Sly, forgets him entirely. What, then, to do with this unwelcome guest?
>
> Some productions omit him completely; some put him in a corner and ignore him; some give him extra 'business' between scenes.
>
> Mr John Barton, Stratford's Assistant Director, now essaying his first solo production, scorns such feeble devices.
>
> Putting on his scholar's robes, he has gone back to an earlier, anonymous version of the play, and from it included extracts, with the purpose, as a programme note tells us, of 'emphasising that the "play-within-a-play" was acted by strolling players for the entertainment of a drunken tinker'.
>
> And 'emphasising' is a word clearly dear to Mr Barton's heart. He apparently imagines that without help from him Shakespeare could never live through to the last act.
>
> But the result is that he not only kills Shakespeare stone dead but shovels the earth over him and stamps it down.
>
> . . . Though Sly, for most of Mr Barton's play, has nothing to do or say, the actors bow to him as they enter and exit, and he 'reacts' with appropriate cries, laughs, ums, ers, gurgles, snorts and gestures.
>
> But there is no order or pattern to this: frequently they ignore Sly and he them.
>
> If we are going to have silly theories ruining Shakespeare could we not at least have them consistently applied?[11]

In an extraordinary abuse of the critic's authority, Levin simply

[31]

missed the entire point of the production. More acute observers were aware that the interpolation of *A Shrew* and the foregrounding of the Sly-frame altered or adjusted both the structure of the play, and its relationship with its audience. Kenneth Tynan defended both the scholarly and theatrical motives of the director:

> John Barton's direction is full of wideawake scholarship . . . As soon as the Induction is over, Shakespeare abandons his gullible tinker; Mr Barton keeps him on stage throughout, and justifies his presence by borrowing lines from the non-Shakespearean *Taming of A Shrew* in which Sly staggers off at the end to practise on his wife what Petruchio has preached.
>
> The device works splendidly, 'framing' the play as its author never did. Inside the frame there is some lovely, jocular acting from a predominantly youthful company . . .[12]

Tynan did not develop this response: and other reviewers found quite correctly that the Sly-frame's introduction of a double perspective created for the performers problems of a dramatic and theoretical kind. Where is the dramatic truth of the play to be found: in the taming-story itself or in the fictive presentation of the Elizabethan players? 'Clearly Mr Barton's object in this his first production at Stratford . . . is to make it perfectly obvious all through that this is a play within a play. Whether the point is worth labouring is another matter . . .'[13] Gareth Lloyd-Evans concluded by contrast that the point was worth labouring, since the theatricality of the frame threw the play proper into an environment of 'bustling, bubbling comic licence':

> By a deliberate marriage of Shakespeare's text with that of an anonymous play, *The Taming of a Shrew* . . . the director has been able to preserve intact the sense of a play-within-a-play.
>
> In part, this leads to some illogicality of movement – Sly has constantly to move from interior to exterior, and vice-versa, in order to keep tabs on Petruchio and Kate. But this is mitigated by the over-all sense of a play put on for the doubtful benefit of a tipsy tinker and a whimsy [*sic*] Lord.[14]

That 'over-all sense' was recognised by some observers as a fundamental determinant of the mood and tone of the whole production, which became visible as a self-reflective performance rather than an Aristotelian action:

> It is a play within a play, acted for the benefit of Sly, who does not comprehend but considers it all a dream. And for two and a half hours the Stratford stage is populated by a company of travelling

[32]

players, with Prompter, acting out the comedy of Kate and Petruchio as they would have done in Elizabethan days. The wonder of the production is that this idea and the atmosphere that surrounds it have been completely realised.

All the conglomerate company are giving a performance as if they are [no] more professional than the hilarious rude mechanicals of Shakespeare's 'Pyramus and Thisby' in *A Midsummer Night's Dream*; they are also as uproarious. For this is a gay production, unashamed of its brashness, full of vigour, rollicking along over the impossibilities of the story, yet faithful to the playwright's intent.[15]

The most sensible critical opinion came from the *Wolverhampton Express and Star* (an instance of acute provincial judgement contrasting appositely with Bernard Levin's abrogation of centralised metropolitan authority) which recognised that the foregrounding of the Sly-frame actually induced a double awareness on the part of the actors, pushing the meaning of the taming fable in the direction of playful fictiveness:

From the beginning, both Katherina, the Shrew, and Petruchio, the Tamer, are themselves aware that their supposed fight is an unreal joke and are conducting it with a twinkle in the eye . . . This Petruchio can do his wife-starving and browbeating without losing our sympathy because he is so obviously playing a sprite-like game that will make Katherina happier in the end.[16]

In fact it does not necessarily follow – as the contrasting instance of Di Trevis's 1985 production, discussed below, will sufficiently indicate – that a visible Sly-frame will necessarily project the inner play into a mood of cheerful, light-hearted playfulness. Such effects depend on a range of additional factors, including casting, acting, direction and the shaping power of institutional and ideological contexts. Moreover, a certain flexibility in the varying emphases given to Sly – the very flexibility which seemed to several critics to amount to inconsistency – allowed for the possibility of long passages in which the doubleness of perspective could be suspended, and the 'playfulness' temporarily perceived as deriving not from the metadramatic structure, but from the specific character of the relationship between tamer and tamed. In a sentimental review celebrating the production's evocation of 'an older and almost forgotten England relived before one's eyes', Robert Speaight indicated that for him the production's virtue was its willingness to vary the centrality accorded to Sly's participation:

Some producers dislike Sly so much that they cut him out altogether;

this has actually been done at Stratford. Others have him acted for considerably more than he is worth. But Mr Barton and Mr McGowran tactfully fade him in and out. He is very much there at the beginning, and rather touchingly so at the end. The play is over; the actors have changed and are off to their next one-night stand; and Mr McGowran wanders in their wake ... This was magnificent, though it was not Shakespeare; the perfect end to an irreproachable evening.[17]

The complacency of this response, the absence from it of any quality of disturbance or ideological challenge, suggests that a flexible Sly-frame may ultimately leave the barbaric ideology that the play works on immune from any serious interrogation or subversion. In much the same way Adrian Noble's now-famous 'post-Falklands' production of *Henry V* (RSC, 1985) foregounded the Chorus, with a Brechtian emphasis, far more than usual; and yet eliminated the Chorus's perspective from those passages in the play through which a reactionary heroic and militaristic ideology may be secured. Barton's *Shrew* similarly brought Sly to a new prominence, only to marginalise his role in the shaping of the play's theatrical ideology.

III

In sharp contrast to those productions (such as Zeffirelli's and Miller's) which derive their visual style and design from the play's Italianate setting, Barton and set-designer Alix Stone chose to model their set on the generic and geographical properties of the 'Induction'. The inn from which the drunken tinker is ejected, embodied in the form of a thatched Tudor hostelry, became the basis for what was in effect a permanent set, around which all the action was played. The newly-installed revolve stage made possible one basic change, from exterior to interior locations. To maintain Sly as a visible observer through a revolving set-change necessitated some ingenuity of movement between scenes – a compromise with the flexibility of Elizabethan staging methods which some critics found irritating (see, for example, Lloyd-Evans, *Stratford Herald*, 24 June 1960); and the large space occupied by the set forced the action downstage towards the audience. This *Shrew* evidently derived much of its comic and metadramatic quality from its centralising of the forestage; though this layout might

[34]

also have helped to marginalise the role of Sly, often seated at some distance from the action, as semi-permanent observer.

> The revolving stage is used and most of it is filled by a permanent set – an inn complete with staircases, balcony, yard and rooms – and for most of the play the actors are confined to only a segment of the circle. With so little freedom their antics are inclined to look clumsy . . .
> The play, which is very much seen as part of the dream of Christopher Sly, is set in a revolving tumbledown barnyard; not very pretty to the eye but at least having the merit of bringing the players well forward among us.[18]

The theatrical space provided by this structure (see illustration 2) afforded an interesting combination of influences. The set contained the basic physical properties of the Elizabethan public theatre's architectural structure: a flat playing area with immediate access to the audience, a façade with two doors, a form of 'gallery' above the stage. The thatched roof of the simulated Tudor inn inevitably echoes the thatched 'hut' that surmounted the stage of the early Elizabethan playhouses. The playing area 'aloft' that was afforded by the Renaissance 'gallery' was in this set dispersed across a number of different spaces – terraces, balconies, windows – from which Sly and other observers from among the cast could act as surrogate 'spectators'. Thus the physical significance of the set was rooted in the geographical and historical location of the Induction: the action was performed unmistakably in and before a Warwickshire Tudor inn by a troupe of players: the Italianate context was signalled only emblematically by nameplates hung over the stage doors – 'Signor Baptista', 'Signor Hortensio'.

Clearly John Barton's scholarly interest in the archaeology of the Elizabethan theatre, and in previous experiments in the attempted reconstruction of such spaces, was in part responsible for the structure and shape of this design. That interest, it should be recognised, was more than merely antiquarian: since it had issued, during Barton's academic career at Cambridge, in some experiments with a quasi-Elizabethan touring theatre group known as the 'Elizabethan Theatre Company', which attempted to revive the theatrical conditions of a travelling ensemble playing in such available locations as could be found 'on the road'.[19] The basic principle of playing a fictional action in front of a visual setting which does not in any realist or naturalistic sense complement the imagined world of the fiction derives from a serious study of the play's originating theatrical architecture.

But a crucial distinction arises here, analogous to the distinction between an attempt at the physical reconstruction or replication of an earlier theatre – a project currently under way on London's Bankside in the form of the International Shakespeare Globe Trust's plan to rebuild the Globe Theatre – and the construction of a theatrical space which will provide the basic physical properties of an antique theatre, without concealing the contemporary process of reconstruction – which may be exemplified by Stratford's Swan. For Barton's Warwickshire inn did not simply return the play to a physical space appropriate to its dramatic rhythms and structures: but rather displayed to the audience a reconstruction of an Elizabethan world, grouped naturalistically around the dominant image of the thatched and rambling Gothic inn. A bare, undecorated space leaves a play entirely to its own devices, forcing it back on to its intrinsic and historically-inscribed rhythms: where Barton's set provided for the play a visual background which consisted, I will argue, of an atavistic image of the past conceived as 'Old' (or even 'Merry') 'England'.[20]

A third element of cultural influence will complete the continuum of Barton's intellectual heritage, and locate it firmly into that powerful Cambridge tradition that has had such an extraordinary shaping control over the dominant structures of the British theatre. We have considered the inheritance of textual scholarship and criticism which led to the Hall–Barton emphasis on the verbal and auditory systems of Elizabethan blank verse – amalgamating influences which were actually antagonistic and contradictory, in the 'practical criticism' of Leavis and in the preoccupation with verse-speaking as a 'craft'. The interest in Elizabethan staging conditions was just as much a product of Cambridge, flowing naturally from the theatre history of Muriel Bradbrook.[21] The third element is a particular version of Renaissance history, which we can still examine, powerfully embodied in the work of Tillyard and John Dover Wilson and which was partly constructed from the historiographical work of now largely discredited historians such as Trevelyan. This involved the strategic reconstruction of the Tudor period as a lost Golden Age of organic community and cultural harmony. This polemical sociology of the past came in a sophisticated and powerful form: yet from the perspective of the present it often seems as naive as the Shakespeare tea-towels and Anne Hathaway cream-buns of the Stratford tourist industry. The set-design for Barton's *Shrew* can now be seen clearly as a crystallisation of that nostalgically-regretted organic past: so that the overall sense of harmony and comic reconciliation provoked by the production was realised within the secure environment of a Tillyardian reconstitution of the imagined harmony of a vanished Old England.[22]

Several reviewers emphasised the 'Elizabethan' quality of the production: 'It is a play full of comic spirit and has that broadness of dialogue and action which the Elizabethan delighted in' (*Yorkshire Post*, 22 June 1960); 'My guess is that the Elizabethans would have been more at home last night than at a cotton-wool production.'[23] Others offered more specific appreciations of the 'medieval' effects: 'the settings strike a mellow medieval note, with a huddled hamlet of timber, plaster and thatch' (*Evening Standard*, 22 June 1960). The *Shakespeare Quarterly* review, already quoted, compressed all these elements into a celebration of the production's medieval qualities; thus confirming the success of the production in *naturalising* the play's contents, not (as Zeffirelli or Bogdanov might do) into a contemporary idiom, but into the transhistorical continuity of immanent human experience embodied in the organic myths of Old England or of the European Middle Ages:

> This is the *Shrew* that Shakespeare drew, tracing its pedigree right down from Chaucer and Langland, and from the carvings that a curious eye may discover on the choir-stalls of an English, or French, cathedral. For the assumptions which lie behind *The Taming of the Shrew* were still common to all Europe; we find them in Villon and Rabelais, as well as in Ben Jonson, just as we catch their later echoes in Molière . . . . (Speaight, p. 447)

IV

A focus on the *actors* in this production almost inevitably entails a primary focus on the leading players, Peter O'Toole and Peggy Ashcroft. Peter Hall's permanent company had not yet been established; it is questionable, given the facts about the long-term contracts discussed earlier, whether a grouping of actors such as that represented by the cast of Barton's *Shrew* ever could have been formulated into an ensemble; and in retrospect the cast of the

Shrew resembles nothing so much as one of the old Shakespeare Memorial Theatre productions of the 1950s, with its mixture of old-stagers, young hopefuls and embryonic stars already aware of the beckoning lights of Hollywood and Broadway. The kind of critical attention given to the production certainly assumed that this basic structure was still in place; and the kind of media curiosity bestowed on the leading actor, Peter O'Toole, represents a phenomenon developed to its extreme in the Burton–Taylor film – a preoccupation with the 'real-life' personalities or relationship of the central 'stars', which are held in some way to exemplify in the public domain the fictional archetypes of the play itself.

The 'real-life'relationship between the twenty-nine-year-old rising star O'Toole and the fifty-two-year-old veteran actress Dame Peggy Ashcroft did not, of course, afford any of the media clichés provoked by the Burton–Taylor coupling in Zeffirelli's *Shrew*. The leading lady received an enthusiastic and respectful star treatment ('She's a perfect shrew at fifty-two'; 'Oh what a Dame!'[24]). But it was her tamer's personal life that lent itself more easily to an identification of actor with role. In a section appropriately entitled 'Limelight', the *Evening Standard* published, shortly after the opening of the *Shrew*, an interview with O'Toole in which the actor obediently proffered an image of unreformed wildness and macho vitality:

> The people who know him well and predict that he may become one of our great actors nearly always add the proviso – if he doesn't destroy himself first.
> 'Oh, yes,' he concedes, 'I get drunk and disorderly and all that. But I don't really think it's true that there is any danger of me destroying myself. I like to make things hum. I like occasionally to shout at the moon and spit at the sun.
> 'How often do I get drunk and smash up the furniture? Oh, not more than three or four times a day.'
> 'What do I get from being drunk? A bloody hangover and grim looks from the missus.'[25]

When encouraged, O'Toole was willing to perform for the interviewer in the character of Petruchio:

> His wife, Sian Phillips, interfered to say that he is not nearly as wild as rumour and invention suggest. If he were she would never have married him.
> 'Rubbish,' bellows Mr O'Toole. 'You couldn't bloody help marrying me.'
> Mrs O'Toole, an actress who has recently played the shrew herself

and has evidently learned the drill, hastily agrees with her husband.

This attribution to an actor of 'star' quality, with the consequent voracity of interest in a personal life which always seems to be another unscheduled performance, has a peculiarly double effect. It can work to separate actor from role, concentrating the spectator's attention on technique: the actor is so well known, the personality so well displayed and publicised, that the 'real' person is always visible beneath whatever dramatic part is being assumed. On the other hand, what appear to be assiduous attempts to foreground a genuine individual personality almost always succeed only in constructing another role: the person is always buried in the fictionalisation of the moment, or absorbed in the public role of actor. Comments on O'Toole's acting in the contemporary critical reviews stress both a mastery of technique and an assured naturalism of presentation. He is seen as playing Petruchio, with comic verve and psychological conviction; but also as playing the actor who plays Petruchio, with an appropriately self-conscious doubleness:

> It is fascinating to compare the techniques of these two artists, the one at her zenith, the other on the brink of greatness. Mr O'Toole begins on a note of rasping exasperation, an overbearing player throwing himself into the declamatory part of the loutish fortune hunter and proceeds with ease, from climax to climax, a fiery crescendo of a performance.[26]

This style of acting, if consistently sustained, would complement the self-reflexive doubleness of the 'framed' production. In the event, O'Toole appears not to have been able to establish sufficient sense of contradiction between performer and role to maintain that necessary doubleness. After all, what lay behind the swaggering braggadocio of his characteric was the swaggering braggadocio of another assumed character, the angry young thespian of the late fifties, the Jimmy Porter of the footlights. The 'real' personality of Petruchio, only lightly masked by the patriarchal bully – good-humoured, sensitive, loveable – fuses effortlessly with the 'star' personality of the actor, naturalising both into a single integrated dimension of ideologically *acceptable* performance:

> Mr O'Toole, with the commanding stage presence of a matinee idol uncamouflaged, does not see Petruchio as merely a thick-skinned goon who must have his own way, but as a man intelligent enough not to sit down under fate and human enough to be mightily relieved

when his sabre rattling works. His strength makes Katherina surrender; his sensitivity makes her want to. (*Wolverhampton Express and Star*, 22 June 1960)

Praise was also bestowed on Peggy Ashcroft's assurance of technique; and in her case the personality that visibly shadowed the performance was that of an experienced actress at the height of her powers, putting in a virtuoso performance in a role not entirely suited to her age or her talents. What was expected of her, and what reviewers agreed she provided, was a combination of admirable technique and psychological conviction:

> Dame Peggy Ashcroft's wish to play a part which she has never played before may be called a whim in the sense that it is a part which runs against the grain of her temperament. She is not naturally at ease in the rough and tumble of farce and it may be for her sake that the play had to be slanted towards comedy. But this actress has a way of brilliantly justifying her whims. She does not in this instance spare the shrewishness, and she is indeed a woe-begone figure at the height of her ordeal.[27]

Once these strategies of identification have accomplished the collapsing of actor into role, of 'player' into 'character', of self-conscious alienation-effect into naturalistic method, it remains only to celebrate the success of the actors in portraying convincing types of realistic human behaviour.

> Peggy Ashcroft makes the shrew a passionate woman of some humour who is fed up to distraction with neglect and basically much taken with Petruchio.
> When she resists him, a twitch of amusement hovers about her mouth. Her suffering before the submission is therefore nominal and fit to joke about; the submission itself is easily swallowed dramatically, and the whole effect is happier and kinder. (*Wolverhampton Express and Star*. 22 June 1960)

> Mr Peter O'Toole gives Dame Peggy just the support her Katherina needs. He uses no whip, and shows no particle of ill-humour, and when he comes in mad attire to the wedding he comes cheerfully blowing bagpipes. It is the purpose of his Petruchio to show how a man of spirit may get the better of a woman of spirit. (*The Times*, 22 June 1960)

> Peter O'Toole's Petruchio is a creature of grace, fire and flashes of gentleness ... The keynote of their interpretation of tamer and tamed is fiery respect growing into immense love. It is as if the challenge thrown down by this vixen lady leads, not so much to cowed captivity, as to a release in the victim of hidden gentleness,

[40]

and, in the victor, of courteous adoration. (Lloyd-Evans. *Stratford Herald*, 24 June 1960)

Her Kate is a raging hoyden who with every shrug, every pout, every word, suggests that behind the habitual mask of the shrew, there breathes a woman simply dying to be . . . tamed. (*Daily Mail*, 22 June 1960)

Each of these critical comments closes the circle of ideological compliance by transforming the taming plot into a love story. Despite the production's promotion, through the framing device of a double awareness and a critical perspective, and the partial complementing of that technique by some self-reflexive acting, O'Toole and Ashcroft succeeded in presenting an irresistibly sympathetic and psychologically convincing portrayal of a couple effectively negotiating the ordeals of conflict to win a harmonious reconciliation. The duping of Christopher Sly became the duping of a Stratford audience. Kenneth Tynan made the production sound, both in terms of its overriding naturalism and its reactionary sexual politics, like a rehearsal for Jonathan Miller's:

Peggy Ashcroft . . . is no striding virago, no Lady Macbeth *manquée*; instead, we have a sulky, loutish girl who has developed into a school bully and a family scold in order to spite Bianca, the pretty younger sister who has displaced her as father's favourite daughter. Her fury is the product of neglect; Petruchio's violence, however extreme, is at least attentive. He cares, though he cares cruelly, and to this she responds, cautiously blossoming until she becomes what he wants her to be. The process is surprisingly touching, and Dame Peggy plays the last scene, in which the rival husbands lay bets on their wives' obedience, with an eager, sensible radiance that almost prompts one to regret the triumph of the suffragette movement. (Tynan, *Observer*, 26 June 1960)

Both the choice of a self-reflexive 'play-within-play' style, and the dominance in both theatrical and ideological dimensions of the leading characters/players, had their influence on the conduct of the Bianca plot. The (relatively) 'minor' characters were presented, more consistently than were the principals, as *actors*, belonging to and defined by the context of the Elizabethan troupe of travelling players. As such they were conceived as professional entertainers equipped with broadly popular but specialised performing skills; while sharing in the general tone of robust and riotous farce, the supporting players offered their roles as, and were universally received as, stock characters from theatrical history. Thus Biondello was a standard acrobatic tumbler, and Gremio a stock pantaloon.

> Dinsdale Landon as Biondello is deliberately grotesque – a fantastic tumbling, grimacing clown, no doubt employed by every Elizabethan travelling company. (Lloyd Evans, *Stratford Herald*, 24 June 1960)

> Farce is the order of the day, and a very lively high-spirited, quick-mettled farce it is. It ranges from another of Patrick Wymark's slow-talking, moon-faced loons, to Paul Hardwick's excellently judged comic timing as Baptista. It takes in Dinsdale Landon's [Biondello's] *commedia dell'arte* clowning, and Ian Holm's whey-faced mouthing as the ancient Gremio.[28]

Barton's adaptation of the Bianca plot thus augmented and accelerated the farcical elements of the production, and threw the central concept of the Elizabethan acting company into visible relief. It did not, paradoxically, intensify and complicate the production's metadramatic dimension: the minor characters threw themselves too vigorously and absolutely into the stock comedy of their roles to achieve any self-reflexive subversion of theatrical illusion. Rather than operating to disclose the deceptive fantasy of the taming plot, the Bianca plot was pushed into relative insignificance by the prominence and relative depth of the leading characters' performances; to many observers it appeared weak or irrelevant:

> For the most part the subsidiary characters stand around in various states of alarm and open admiration, like shelterers in a doorway watching a spectacular thunderstorm.[29]

> The virtuosity of these two artists tends to expose the sub-plot for the feeble and tired thing it is. While it is in progress one physically aches for them to reappear. (*Daily Mail*, 22 June 1960)

V

Those of us who either do not share such a prompted regret that the suffragette movement has triumphed, or would question the very assumption that it has, will need to ponder carefully on the sexual politics of Barton's production. An initial hypothesis can be drawn from a contemporary review: 'It may be a gratifying joke to suggest that the best cure for a shrew is to starve her of food and sleep until she calms down – but it is also an unkind one. John Barton's production . . . draws the sting from the unkindness and applies the soothing balm of sophisticated humanity' (*Wolverhampton Express and Star*, 22 June 1960). This comment suggests that Barton's evident desire to return the play to a context analogous to the conditions of its originating historical moment, unlike the parallel ambition of Jonathan Miller's production, did not envisage any serious revaluation of the play's more recent theatrical traditions. Where Miller saw a fundamental divergence between the Elizabethan attitudes of the play towards women, marriage, the family, and whatever modern 'sophisticated humanity' may have to say about these matters, Barton assumed an underlying continuity. Where Miller sought to establish a sharp contrast between the ideology of the play and modern sensibilities, and between his production and the play's theatrical traditions, Barton was content both to revive the play as a high-spirited farce, and to retain in place those romantic and sentimental appropriations of the taming plot which deliver it as a playful and energetic love-story. In place of whatever views on the nature of women underpinned the taming plot in its original dramatic form, Barton's production (in keeping with many others) supplied a sub-text consisting of, as the dominant motives of the tamer, genial good-humour, powerful sexual attraction and genuine solicitude; and as the defining characteristics of the shrew, a serious family and social problem of alienation and arrested adolescence, a strong and spontaneous response to the vitality and masculinity of the tamer, and a willingness to submit the energies of resistance to the man who offers an attentive regime of caring concern, of however unusual a kind. One reviewer deployed, with an almost touching naivety, the full armour of misogynist metaphor, to argue that the production actually worked to celebrate the dignity of women:

> [Peggy Ashcroft's] appearance conveys nothing of the virago, her voice is not that of the nagger, and there is nothing vixenish about her. She attempts none of these things with her Katherina, but rather conveys the impression of a spirited, wilful, quick-tempered and intractable young girl – conscious of her charms and daring anyone to master her waywardness.
> This is well within her compass and enables the transition to dutiful, obedient and loving wife to be most smoothly and convincingly carried out.
> This is a performance of skilfully contrived moods, ranging from rebellion, through utter misery, dejection and despair, to final bliss-

ful content, without the slightest loss of dignity. Indeed, Miss Ashcroft's is a Katherina never without dignity and not without humour.

This Katherina is well-matched and mastered by Peter O'Toole's well-controlled Petruchio.

Without undue swagger and braggadocio but with an inspired touch of the fantastic, his is a striking, good-humoured Petruchio, handsome, supremely self-confident, domineering and noisy as occasion demands, but with an underlying good humour.[30]

The sexual vocabulary of this critic's discourse draws from that very inheritance of medieval misogyny which underlies the play itself – shrew, virago, vixen – and poses these demonised terms against the language of legitimacy, derived unsurprisingly from the Christian marriage service – dutiful, obedient, loving. A production that could transform one into the other through a 'smooth' and 'convincing' transition must stand as a paradigm of the principal ideological function of comedy – the fictional reconciliation of real historical contradictions. The production thus appealed to a kind of middle ground of enlightened liberal opinion, capable of embracing both the Chaucerian roughness of the play's action, and the ostensibly egalitarian romance assumed as a norm by most modern spectators. Fundamental to such interpretations of the play is the supplied or imposed premise that Katherina and Petruchio fall 'in love at first sight'. There is of course no overt or self-evident indication in any textual inscription of the play that this should be the case: but given that a production has to define explicitly the nature of the relationship between tamer and victim, the assumption of instantaneous mutual attraction is a perfectly valid and reasonable one. The problem that arises from that premise is that the entire process of taming becomes either a strategically-executed process of psychiatric therapy, which we can endorse and approve only if we accept (a) that the patient stands in genuine need of such treatment, and (b) that the motives and methods of the tamer are reliable, trustworthy, well-intentioned and evidently in the best interests of the patient; or it becomes an elaborate game, played out between tamer and tamed, on the basis of a tacit understanding between them that their observable behaviour will never quite reveal to their observers the truth of their personalities or their relationship. The most well-known rendering of the first premise is Miller's TV production; the classic instance of the latter interpretation is Zeffirelli's film. Barton's production occupied a terrain somewhere between these two versions. Peggy Ashcroft's realisation of Katherina certainly suggested that she needed help; Peter O'Toole's playing of Petruchio left the audience in little doubt that his intentions were, beneath the swaggering façade, honourable; and his motives, behind the economic opportunism, charitably philanthropic:

> If the *Shrew* is to succeed, it is essential that we should like Petruchio and Katherina, and that they should be seen to like each other. It is not easy to dislike Dame Peggy, even when she is cudgelling her sister, and she made it clear to us, in a flash of fine acting, that she had fallen in love with Petruchio at first sight. There is a tenderness and humour underneath these tantrums and this tyranny, a certain Shakespearean delicacy, which the exigencies of farce had not been able to dispel and which these two performers marvellously disclosed. (Speaight, p. 447)

The 'likeableness' of the actors, a feature of the production evidently enhanced rather than diminished by the double perspective of the framing effect, ensured a sympathetic presentation of the process of taming. While some reviewers cautiously postulated an egalitarian sub-text, others openly celebrated the production's declaration of a reactionary sexual politics. This could take the form of portentous generalisation, formulated in suitably antique language – with even an echo of Jane Austen: '. . . Because it has for its theme a truth universally acknowledged that a woman of spirit may be glad to meet her master and may be at odds with the world until she does so, this play can be made to yield something that transcends pure farce.'[31] Or in a more open confrontation with contemporary ideology, Milton Shulman appreciated the production as definitively 'anti-feminist'. Clearly, although the production made available a range of different readings, from liberal to reactionary, there is in the recorded responses of spectators a consensus that it operated to legitimise the ideology of 'taming' as a valid principle in male–female relationships. Given that legitimation, the overtly anti-feminist language of what follows must seem a deserved, and possibly entirely appropriate, formulation:

> There is no quibbling about this production . . . it is a complete and anti-feminist version of this boisterous and rowdy Shakespearean comedy.
> . . . Other productions have tended to soften this humiliating demonstration of man's mastery over women. By a gesture or a wink or a cynical chirp in the voice, Kate's final submissive speeches have indicated that her surrenders are merely tactical and that in the long run she will again be the boss.

[45]

But last night there were no such reservations. In Peter O'Toole we have the most aggressive, virile, dominating Petruchio in years. Any woman who stood in his way would be blown apart by a puff or a sneeze. It is a marvellously comic performance which will put heart into even the most brow-beaten husband in the audience.

Against such a whirlwind of masculine ego even so sturdy an actress as Peggy Ashcroft can but yield and surrender.

There is no doubt that women's suffrage suffers a considerable beating in the completeness of her capitulation. (*Evening Standard*, 22 June 1960)

VI

I have observed on several occasions in the preceding pages that the emphasis on innocuous playfulness that seemed to derive from Barton's use of the Sly-framework was neither a necessary nor a predictable effect of that theatrical structure. This point can be demonstrated, and a further sustained contrast with the Barton production suggested, by a brief discussion of a production very different in style, genre and ideological emphasis: directed, perhaps significantly, by a woman, Di Trevis. This was a Royal Shakespeare Company touring production of 1985, toured in tandem with Brecht's *Happy End*.[32] The juxtaposition was clearly not fortuitous, since the Shakespearean production was itself very Brechtian. The travelling players of Shakespeare's text were foregrounded as a group of nineteenth-century actors, evidently poor and oppressed: the opening scene showed the actress who was to play Katherina pulling a cart in the style of Mother Courage. Not only was Christopher Sly kept on stage throughout as a constant choric presence, but the production maintained a constant awareness of the actors as players performing. Sly functioned consistently as an on-stage observer or surrogate audience of the players' performance; his reactions provided the actual audience with a criterion for measuring and testing their own. It was never entirely possible to forget that the play was clearly being performed by the players. Sly was foregrounded as a desperately poor and hopeless man, a victim of the Lord's capricious pranks, pathetically persuaded that he possesses power and riches. This framing-effect enabled the audience both to estrange and distance the play's events, and to consider them in terms of the realities of poverty and power.

[46]

The Brechtian influence extended beyond the alienation-effect of the Sly-frame to modify also the nature of the acting. In a sharp contrast with the pervasively genial good humour of Barton's production, Trevis's permitted the possibility of distancing and disruption:

> Alfred Molina was not afraid of showing the audience the unpleasant aspects of Petruchio. When he referred to Kate as 'my goods, my chattels', he did not attempt to mitigate the force of the words by speaking them lightheartedly. But neither did he show Petruchio as an unpleasant man, with whom it was unnecessary to sympathise: instead, he spoke the words clearly and strongly, and with a certain integrity, challenging the audience to formulate their own response.[33]

Sly himself appears to have been foregrounded more consistently and given more vigorous powers of intervention than the 'tactful fading in and out' deployed by Barton. The tinker's attempted interruption of the play when Lucentio is threatened with prison was again played as a decisive disruption of the proceedings, but not merely as a comic play, and with a clearer crystallisation of the metadramatic dimension. Sly had evidently himself been 'inside'. The tinker's intervention threw the 'inner play' into relief, and fractured its illusions, reminding the audience unmistakably that they were watching a play. But they were also reminded of Sly's poverty and of his previous narrow brush with the law. Sly himself is revealed as entirely under the sway of theatrical illusion: 'his involvement in the fiction of his role makes him believe in his ability to affect the fictitious events being enacted before him; but his power is as illusory as the play he watches, and as his privileged status' (Cousins, *New Theatre Quarterly*, 2, 1986, p. 281.)

These complementary emphases on fictiveness and on poverty brought a very different focus to the play's denouement. Where Barton's production resolved into reconciliation and harmony, this interpretation sustained the full implications of its metadramatic structure to the end. The taming-story proceeded and ended conventionally enough, with Katherina and Petruchio achieving reconciliation and understanding. The play-within-a-play ended with a wedding; the players took their bows and disappeared. The fiction of the taming plot was over, its illusions established. Under the sway of this sentimental romance, Sly approached his 'lady', evidently believing in the possibility of mutual affection. In a startling denouement, the page threw off his wig and ran away, with a mocking laugh. The realisation that Sly had been less a spectator than an actor in the performance was compounded by the Lord's contemptuously throwing money at his feet. The surrogate spectator is thus left bewildered and lost, unable to integrate or understand his experience of the pleasures of fiction. The actress who had played Katherina then re-entered, holding a baby and looking again downtrodden and burdened. The reconciliation by taming was revealed as a pleasant but groundless pretence, played to delude Sly and satisfy the Lord's caprice. Where Barton's production closed with a triumphant celebration of comic harmony and sentimental romance, Di Trevis's production closes – in a very Brechtian moment – with Sly offering the poor actress a share of the Lord's bounty. The poor man and the poor woman have both been victimised: and in a mutual recognition of that they find both a shared experience and a common cause.

CHAPTER III

Franco Zeffirelli (1966)

Theatre and film are both media of 'performance', yet the technological and theoretical differences between them are radical and profound. I posed in my introductory chapter the by-now familiar distinction between a play as literary textualisation and as living enactment: on the one hand the printed text, apparently permanently fixed and immobile, resistant to intervention or participation, inviting the kind of reading that seeks the intended coherence of authorial meaning; on the other the ephemeral medium of theatrical performance, an experiential form obviously concerned with the shaping of a malleable material, open to contribution from performers and audience alike, a collaborative enterprise of production and interpretation. Film and theatre can be thought of as so naturally complementary that the translation of a play from one to another – the feature film developed from a stage production or the videotape of a live performance – is a smooth and unproblematic process.

In fact the medium of film, at least in terms of the social and cultural uses to which the technology has traditionally been put, has more in common in this context with literature than with drama. Clearly the processes of theatrical and film adaptation have equal liberty to interpret and reconstruct a dramatic text: both theoretically 'free', both subject to the pressures and determinants of any socio-cultural situation. The process by which a 'text' is turned into a 'performance', through analysis, discussion, inter-pretative experiment, improvisation and rehearsal, may be very similar in each case. Yet although in a film a play is being enacted by living performers, that concrete human realisation is over-ridden by the finality of the finished product: the enactment is then fixed and frozen in a perpetually mobile immobility. In a theatrical space actors may be empowered to continue interpret-ing the dramatic text in an experimental process of discovery and improvisation; in a film, whatever procedures of rehearsal and exploration may precede the final shooting, the entire product of the actors' communication is arrested at the point of editing. In a theatre an audience is present at the dramatic event, participating in the performance in whatever manner may be permitted by the nature of the theatrical space and the relations between actors and audience; in a cinema the spectator is present at the image of an absent event, illuminatingly shadowed by the two-dimensional phantasmagoria of the screen.

Of course this distinction deals with potentialities rather than with innate and inevitable characteristics of the respective media. A convention-bound theatrical performance, or one which is choreographed to the point of fossilisation, can approach as closely to the resistant fixity of literature as a naturalistic film; and a more experimental filmic medium can realise in concrete form some of the pluralistic potentialities still present in the discourse of 'script' or 'screenplay'. Having proposed a global theoretical distinction between the two performance media, we can move to a further distinction between conservative and experimental dis-courses within each medium: and within that distinction it is poss-ible to discover a parallel, between the pictorial realism of nineteenth-century staging, and the naturalistic tendency of cer-tain kinds of film.

If the introduction of perspective scenery and pictorial sets was a means of bringing the theatre closer to the representation of reality, then clearly the medium of film immediately outstripped the imitative technology of the stage. Film was able not only to portray reality more convincingly through the use of studio sets: it could also represent physical reality itself directly through loca-tion shooting. Early silent films of Shakespeare plays have been treated by film historians and critics with enormous condescen-sion, as little more than a crude rehearsal for the artistic and technological flowering of the talkies. This misjudgement is a typical undervaluing of the visual elements of drama, and a misunderstanding of the historical development of silent film. For most of the nineteenth century only the privileged patent theatres were permitted to use the verbal texts of serious drama, with the result that elsewhere the theatre had been obliged to develop a primarily visual and musical discourse (*melo-drama*) with which to communicate the plays. Silent film simply appropriated this theatrical language and realised it through a pictorial naturalism of visual style and the deployment of mime techniques in acting.

This historical link between the nineteenth-century pictorial stage and the medium of film has also received theoretical attention. Catherine Belsey has argued that film is 'the final realisation of the project of perspective staging', and that both stand in fundamental confrontation with the theatrical language of the Renaissance public playhouse:

> In the Elizabethan theatre there is no proscenium arch, no painted backdrop defining a setting in perspective, but a stage projected outwards into the auditorium, with the audience placed on at least three sides of it and possibly four. There is no single place to which the action is addressed and from which it is intelligible. The introduction after 1660 of the proscenium theatre with perspective backdrops radically changed the relationship between the audience and the stage . . .
> Film is the final realisation of the project of perspective staging. The framed rectangle contains a world which is set out as the single object of the spectator's gaze, displayed in order to be known from a single point of view . . . Through the intervention of the camera, which monitors what we see and therefore what we know, the film collects up meanings which may be lying around in the text, and streamlines them into one single, coherent interpretation which it fixes as inescapable. It arrests the play of possible meanings and presents its brilliant rectangle full of significance to and from a specific place, a single and at the same time inevitable point of view.[1]

I have argued elsewhere[2] that this fixing of interpretation and privileging of the single point of view is not a *necessary* effect of film, which as a medium has the technological resources to resist such 'textualisation'. It is nonetheless clear that film which invites or endorses complicity with the techniques of the proscenium arch and pictorial stage runs the risk of surrendering from the play those pluralistic capacities guaranteed it by the architectural space of its original performance. It is likely to localise what should be unlocalised; concretise what should be left open to the imagination; represent what should be distanced, and naturalise what should be estranged. Zeffirelli's film version of *The Taming of the Shrew*, best known as a naturalistic and pictorial treatment of the play, requires serious consideration in the terms of this theoretical problem.

The critical discourses available for description, analysis and interpretation of a stage version of a Shakespeare play derive from literary criticism, theatrical reviewing, and specifically dramatic perspectives such as those of theatre history and the semiotics of drama. Performance analysis is as yet in its infancy, not having synthesised these diverse influences into an assured and confident integrated language. A genuinely *filmed* version of a Shakespeare play (as distinct from a filmed stage version) invites interpretative response from film criticism and theory as well as from the literary and dramatic approaches. This conjuncture creates particular difficulties, since the mainstream of film criticism, unlike the methodologies of the other disciplines, is highly theoretical, avant-garde and internationalist, where literary and dramatic criticism tend predominantly to be empirical, conservative and chauvin-istic. Film criticism has thoroughly absorbed the influences of the post-structuralist revolution in cultural theory, and concerns itself with genre studies, popular culture, semiotics; with experimental rather than traditional work; and with cinema as a global language with a world-wide constituency. To many exponents of film criti-cism a film of a Shakespeare play is not truly a film at all, but a hybrid amalgamation of two hostile cultural discourses, tainted by the noxious traces of the stage, of high art, of cultural elitism and of British cultural imperialism. Critical work on Shakespeare films has been produced on that marginal terrain of literary and dramatic studies where film and television are employed in an essentially ancillary manner to support a critical enterprise centred on text and theatrical realisation.

From that marginal space emerge voices articulating cultural contradition and divided loyalty. It has become a commonplace in the criticism of Shakespeare films that the Renaissance play and the filmic medium are radically dissimilar and in some funda-mental ways incompatible. Yet almost all such criticism insists on interpreting and evaluating a Shakespeare film in comparison with the 'original' textual inscription. Starting from the premise that a piece of sixteenth-century dramatic literature fiercely resists translation into a twentieth-century technological medium, critics nonetheless reserve the right to castigate a film for failing to realise

'Shakespeare'. Here, for example, is a formulation of the key distinction between stage and film to which all writers on film would have to assent:

> If Racine, Shakespeare or Molière cannot be brought to the cinema by just placing them before the camera and the microphone, it is because the handling of the action and the style of the dialogue were conceived as echoing through the architecture of the auditorium. What is specifically theatrical about these tragedies is not their action so much as the human, that is to say the verbal, priority given to their dramatic structure. The problem of filmed theatre at least where the classics are concerned does not consist so much in transposing an action from the stage to the screen as in transposing a text written for one dramaturgical system into another while at the same time retaining its effectiveness.[3]

Yet here is a characteristically hostile critique of Zeffirelli's *Taming of the Shrew* which first concedes, and then simply ignores, this distinction:

> True, this is a film, not a play, and must be judged on its own terms, but no one with an understanding of the relation of the parts to the whole in a successful work could effectively hope to make a good film using the playwright's words in so significantly altered a setting.
>
> Zeffirelli's next project is *Romeo and Juliet* as a *ciné-verité* documentary on Renaissance Verona. Which takes us back to the very first point: one can't help feeling that only a man without a concept of the way parts of an art work relate to the whole could cherish this ambition; or a man who neither understands nor profoundly likes Shakespeare for what he is.[4]

Our discussion of this particular example of 'Shakespeare in performance' will thus inevitably be dogged by this theoretical impasse between stage and screen. I will attempt to evaluate Zeffirelli's production in its own specifically *filmic* terms rather than in comparison with some ideal model of an authoritatively Shakespearean realisation.

To think of Zeffirelli purely as a film director is an oversimplification. He began his career studying architecture and stage design in Florence; became first an actor and then a costume- and set-designer in the theatre; worked as a film technician with masters of the Italian cinema such as Luchino Visconti; designed and directed operas; and came to the filming of Shakespeare through successful attempts to direct the plays in the theatre – his other

Shakespeare film *Romeo and Juliet* (1968) began its long gestation as a stage production at the Old Vic in 1960. Recently he has filmed opera with *La Traviata* and designed, directed and filmed Verdi's opera of Shakespeare's *Othello*. It would be difficult to imagine a career better calculated to place a director in the ideal position to make a film of a Shakespeare play. But Zeffirelli's conception of Shakespeare is very unlike that restless curiosity about the intrinsic potentialities of the text and its filmic capacities that we associate with Laurence Olivier or Orson Welles: he appears more inclined towards a European's formal respect for the virtues of classical 'English' theatre. That notion of the classic, its artistic value and moral potency, forms an element in a humanistic aesthetic concerned with the potential unity of European culture. When invited by the Old Vic to direct in England, Zeffirelli confessed to an idealistic view of the project as a synthesis of modern Italian emotions with classical English values:

> I had worked in England presenting Italian works and the real satisfaction I took back to Italy was simply that I had helped a little towards the better understanding of its culture by the English.
>
> Now I have an even more interesting task – a combination of Italian feelings applied to a masterpiece of the classical English theatre whch might prove, if successful, that times have changed in Europe and people of different backgrounds can easily work together for creating a new European conscience.
>
> This is to me far more important than any diplomatic or political manoeuvres.[5]

This liberal–humanist internationalism links the cultural theory of an earlier age (manifested most clearly in our own tradition by T. S. Eliot) with the political alliances of a later: an aesthetic superstructure for the Treaty of Rome. Zeffirelli's much-quoted sentiments indicate a number of priorities and preocupations governing his approach to Shakespeare: a formal reverence for the masterpieces of the classical past, which can paradoxically, in its celebration of cultural continuity, involve a lack of interest in the formal properties of those masterpieces; a view of theatrical work as a kind of cultural diplomacy, fostering international understanding and sympathy through the European community; a real concern with a broad popular audience; and a subordination of historical interest in the Elizabethan drama to a vision of its mobilisation in the service of contemporary socio-cultural unity. Where Zeffirelli is deeply interested in history – and this has important implications for his production of the *Shrew* – it is the history of his own Italian culture rather than that of the English Renaissance: to him Shakespeare serves as a bridge between a classical past and the immediate preoccupations of the present.

It is not only as a film-maker therefore that Zeffirelli regarded Shakespeare as fair game for a contemporary appropriation. His naturalistic aesthetic (owing more to the 'neo-realist' *ciné-verité* of Italian movies than to the traditional fictional or theatrical realisms of Zola and Giovanni Verga) is directed firmly towards a rendering of the classical heritage into forms immediate and comprehensible to modern experience. This aspiration involved a particular emphasis on the young, both as participants and spectators: since it was contemporary youth that Zeffirelli hoped to engage as an audience for both his theatrical and film productions. His film of *Romeo and Juliet* stands as the most obvious example of an attempt to communicate directly with young people through a drama of adolescent passion: casting the teenagers Leonard Whiting and Olivia Hussey as the lovers, Zeffirelli subordinated his respect for the classical virtues to a naturalistic emphasis on identification and vicarious experience. When John Francis Lane visited the set of *The Taming of the Shrew* in Rome during the making of the film, he found himself 'intruding on an undergraduate "rag", the type of student jamboree which has been a feature of university life in all Europe's seats of learning from the Middle Ages to the 1960s'.[6] Though the *Shrew* is based on a stock 'New Comedy' situation involving conflict between generations, it is hardly a drama of teenage passion and misunderstanding: so the mobilisation of adolescent masses for this play was evidently symptomatic of Zeffirelli's insistence on communicating the play to a youthful audience. The undergraduate 'rag' became the film's opening sequence: in order to compose it Zeffirelli recruited the fashionably disaffected adolescents of Rome for a crowd scene. He advertised in local papers inviting the local *capelloni* (literally 'long-haired ones') to come for auditions, and transformed them into the undergraduates of Renaissance Padua.

> Zeffirelli conceived the film as a bridge between Renaissance Italy and Elizabethan England; but also between the lusty ribald way of life of those times and the no less vigorous 'swinging' world of our own day. the kids who let off steam in fifteenth-century Padua are shown to be just as full of spirits as the lads and lasses of Pope Paul's Rome or Harold Wilson's London. It is not surprising to learn

that Zeffirelli's favourite film of last year was not one of the sacred masterpieces of Jean-Luc Godard. It was *Help!* (Lane, pp., 51-2)

The Italianising of Shakespeare which earned the director the ironical title of 'Shakespirelli' ('What Zeffirelli is aiming at is to restore the Italian Renaissance spirit to Shakespeare', Lane, p. 52) goes hand in hand with a determined spirit of modernisation: Zeffirelli's 'Pop-Shakespeare' productions were designed to speak to a younger generation as eloquently as the Beatles' film *Help!* According to John Francis Lane, this ambition was clearly being realised: 'Above all, the young Italians are packing the playhouses to see his Shakespeare productions. Some youngsters who had never seen Shakespeare before . . . are startled to find that Shakespirelli's Romeo and Juliet behave like two young people of today' (Lane, p. 52).

These are some of the reasons why Zeffirelli's film versions of Shakespeare are probably among the most enduringly popular of such productions. The other obvious reasons have little to do with youth, and more with Zeffirelli's success in organising the 'production' side of the film, integrating it firmly into the power-structure of the cinema industry. The economic buoyancy of the entire project compares interestingly with Orson Welles' protracted and impoverished struggles to make, for example, *Othello*: and this favourable commercial climate for the *Shrew* evidently owed much to the wealthy and successful 'stars' of the film, Richard Burton and Elizabeth Taylor, who also acted as co-producers, investing over $3,000,000. Richard Roud of the *Guardian* reflected ironically on the cultural–commercial alliances that formed the infrastructure of this particular realisation of Shakespeare on film:

> When the Carnegies and the Rockefellers had all made their packets, their thoughts began to turn to culture. They built libraries, founded foundations, and created cultural centres. This is a recognised pattern in America, and one that is even encouraged by the tax laws. So it would be churlish to reproach the Burtons – Richard and Elizabeth – for simply having followed the custom of their adopted country. After the *Butterfield 8*s, the *Cleopatra*s, they now can offer us *Dr Faustus*, possibly even a *Romeo and Juliet*. This week we are faced with the first of their cultural enterprises for the cinema: *The Taming of the Shrew*.[7]

Both *The Taming of the Shrew* and *Romeo and Juliet* were premiered, in 1966 and 1968, as Royal Command Performances before, respectively, Princess Margaret and Her Majesty the Queen.

[56]

II

It could occasion little surprise, in view of Zeffirelli's credentials as a naturalistic director, that he would find no use for Shakespeare's 'Induction' or the Christopher Sly framework: as Jack Jorgens observes, 'Whatever ironic perspective Shakespeare provided by making the main action a crude entertainment for a drunken, deluded tinker trying in vain to get his "wife" into bed is gone, for like many theatrical directors, Zeffirelli has omitted the framestory altogether'.[8] In its place Zeffirelli supplied his own 'induction', in the form of the fifteenth-century 'student rag' described above. Jack Jorgens describes the opening sequence:

> *Padua.* Lucentio and Tranio ride through lush countryside, arriving in busy Renaissance city. Occupied with a huge blonde whore, Tranio loses his master in the crowd. Titles over university choir singing sombre music, students being blessed in a cathedral. Festive music as students run wild in streets in masks, waving banners, conducting mock funeral, mimicking blonde Bianca as she is bawdily serenaded by gallants: 'Give me leave/ To do for thee all that Adam did for Eve.' Bianca, summoned home, is chased by Lucentio and Tranio, Gremio and Hortensio. (Jorgens, p. 259)

Thus the film modulates into the first of its many farcical chases – it ends with Petruchio still chasing an irrepressibly escaping Kate – via the dramatisation of a ritual of celebration considerably older than (though conjecturally the ancestor of) the 1960s undergraduate 'rag'. The collapse of an ecclesiastical service into merciless parody (the 'mock funeral'), unrestrained revelry and orgiastic release is Zeffirelli's attempt to reconstruct the carnivals of the Middle Ages. Our contemporary rediscovery of the cultural theory of Mikhail Bakhtin[9] has made 'carnival' a key concept in the analysis of all medieval and Renaissance dramatic art: Zeffirelli simply tapped the resources of his own national history to produce a detailed evocation of saturnalian ritual. In the course of the opening sequence (framed as an 'induction' by the superimposition of film titles), we observe the barbaric anti-ceremony of clerics wearing grotesque animal masks, sacred music giving way to obscene and cacophonous chants, a blasphemously parodic image of the Virgin. This ritualistic subversion of hierarchy and orthodoxy is

[57]

a visually powerful and historically detailed dramatisation of those medieval festivals of misrule conjecturally derived from the saturnalian rituals of Rome. An appropriate source is provided by the well-known description by a Parisian academic writing in 1445:

> Who, I ask you, with any Christian feelings, will not condemn when priests and clerks are seen wearing masks and monstrous visages at the hours of Office: dancing in the choir, dressed as women, panders or mistrels, singing lewd songs? They eat black-pudding at the horn of the altar next the celebrant, play at dice there, censing with foul smoke from the soles of old shoes, and running and leaping about the whole church in unblushing, shameless iniquity; and then, finally, they are seen driving about the town and its theatres in carts and deplorable carriages to make an infamous spectacle for the laughter of bystanders and participants, with indecent gestures of the body and language most unchaste and scurrilous.[10]

The elements of parody and subversion, the substitution of license for restraint, obscenity for virtue, the orgiastic celebration of the material body for the metaphysical rituals of the Mass, are here correctly identified as a form of drama – an 'infamous spectacle' for the entertainment of bystanders. Carnival is not simply release or escape from restraint and discipline: it is a temporary period of sanctioned licence, in which a permitted overthrow of established hierarchy is enacted through parodic rituals which do not, despite their appearance of anarchy and liberation, escape from the formal character of ritual. The medieval church allowed such temporary suspensions of order, just as Rome permitted its slaves their day of privilege and supremacy, not from any commitment to liberty and popular rule, but as a means of channelling subversive energy into acceptable and assimilable forms.[11]

By jettisoning the Sly-frame Zeffirelli may in the opinion of some observers have been indicating his contempt for his 'original'. But unlike Jonathan Miller's television version, which omitted the 'Induction' altogether, or the same director's subsequent RSC production (which simply replaced the 'Induction' with musical interludes performed by some pointlessly happy *commedia dell'arte* morris-dancers) Zeffirelli has sought and found an alternative establishing context which is at once an educated and intelligent historical reconstruction and a brilliant initial exposé of the production's principles of interpretation. Jack Jorgens has effectively analysed the relationship between induction and denouement:

This rowdy procession with its chaos of shouts, songs, and shrieks of laughter disrupts the daily routine in Padua, routs seriousness and pretensions to dignity, overturns the hierarchies of power, and dissolves boredom and drudgery. It challenges the populace, tests their sexual prowess, creative energy, thirst, appetites, and late-night endurance. It renews communal feelings by replacing social and economic competition with an orgy of hospitality. Part of the idyll is that modern urban paranoia is banished and creative anarchy reigns, cementing the society together and making life – fraught as it is with failure, sickness, and death – more tolerable. (Jorgens, pp. 74-5)

The function of carnival is to promote social integration: the purpose of ritualised disorder to endorse the stability of the order that can afford to permit its own temporary abolition. Such a model of contradiction resolved may well serve as an appropriate pattern for Shakespearean comedy: Kate's subversive energy of resistance and Petruchio's parodic exposure of commercialised relationship both serve ultimately, and paradoxically, to reintegrate the disrupted order of Paduan society; just as the drama that contained and enacted this reintegration functioned as an endorsement of the imposed 'order' of the Tudor state. Zeffirelli's 'Induction' also became, by virtue of the circumstances of its first exhibition, in a sense, self-reflexive: since this boisterous display of Bohemian anarchy and anti-social energy was enacted, like the old festivals of misrule, before representatives of the very authority whose power such rituals are designed to challenge – in this case, the British monarchy.

III

According to Zeffirelli's aesthetic, the sets displayed realism to the last detail. When [John] Stride approached the stage on opening night to get a feel of the sets and lighting, he discovered Zeffirelli flicking a brush with dirty, watery paint about eighteen inches above the floor. 'this is where the dogs pee on the walls', the director explained. Then he flicked a little higher, saying, 'and this is where the men pee'. (Levenson, p. 100)

This anecdote, recalled from the 1960 Old Vic production of *Romeo and Juliet*, displays several characteristics of Zeffirelli as director/ designer: his personal intervention into the labour of the design process; his naturalistic concern with accuracy and fidelity of re-presentation; and his excessively punctilious eye for detail. His links with naturalist conventions colour all his theatrical and film work, both in terms of directing and designing. As we have seen, his 'ciné-verité documentary on Renaissance Verona' cast as principals actors whose youthfulness and inexperience would help to dissolve their personalities into those of the tragic lovers; and as we shall see below, similar motives underlay the casting of Burton and Taylor in the *Shrew*.

But what exactly constitutes naturalism in terms of movie design? Zeffirelli's sets for the 1960 *Romeo and Juliet* were easily recognisable as a familiar formulation of theatrical conventions, deriving ultimately from the pictorial perspective stages of the nineteenth-century theatre. Naturalism in the cinema was associated, certainly in Zeffirelli's immediate cultural context, with the location shooting and sharp black-and-white photography of films like de Sica's *Bicycle Thieves*, the cinematic equivalent of Zola's scientific novel. The filmic naturalism of Zeffirelli's movies has much more in common with the highly-coloured and decorative realism of Visconti's historical films, where realism has taken on the glowing tints of historical painting rather than the stark monochrome of documentary film. It is this historical realism, framed always by the pervasive influences of visual art, that constitutes the primary medium of *The Taming of the Shrew*. *Romeo and Juliet* was filmed in a wide variety of locations throughout Italy, since Zeffirelli wanted to fill his screen with the concrete reality of Renaissance city streets, churches and palaces, wooded hillsides and romantic balconies.[12] The *Shrew* was filmed entirely in the de Laurentiis studies in Rome.

As far as Zeffirelli is concerned, a director is responsible also for design: and possibly his training as an artist made it inevitable that he should visualise a production with a painter's eye. That visualisation was not simply a matter of reconstructing an accurate realistic background (down to the dog-pee on the walls) before which the action could be played: it seems to be much more a question of the director–designer's artistic sensibility evoking a design concept from his own reading of the text.

> Although he deliberately adopted this older realist aesthetic – he found it imaginatively stimulating (*The Times*, 19 September 1960) – Zeffirelli also relied on instinct and fantasy. He analysed musical or dramatic texts into images, which he composed in a synthesis

determined not only by his understanding, but also by his emotional response to the work. Like the young Peter Brook, Zeffirelli believed in 'a controlling image, a core'. His image always took visual form, or a painterly design. In a conversation with Laurence Kitchin on the BBC, 11 February 1964, Zeffirelli described the emergence of this image as 'a creative beginning', the sole creative moment for the artist interpreting his subject or the director interpreting his script. What comes after the visualisation simply elaborates it; and in stage design, what follows may involve collaboration with the author.

For Zeffirelli, the stage became a huge canvas on which to produce the impression of a living fresco with paint, fabric, colour, timber. (Levenson, pp. 86-7)

Although the studio sets designed to represent Renaissance Padua were insistently naturalistic – 'Mongiardino's magnificent sets were so perfect that even rainstorms could be reproduced, with the water running downhill, without the cobbled streets of "Padua" looking any worse for wear' (Lane, p. 52) – the overwhelming emphasis was on a pictorial evocation of Renaissance culture, a colourful and chaotic genre-painting which could be galvanised into vitality by the nervous mobility and fluidity of *ciné-verité* camera-work. On the set John Francis Lane discovered cameraman Ossie Morris 'holding a well-thumbed book of Correggio reproductions as he studied the lighting for a shot', and actors 'busily studying books about Venetian art' (Lane, p. 51). Reviewers responded to this 'painterly' quality, often with cross-references, appreciative or critical, to the visual arts:

> The picture is enticing to look at, with a sunny-natured opening scene in a gauzy drizzle, high shots of rapt onlookers and crankily angled passages, brownish tints through the reds, and Burton in a bucolic make-up that looks like a Venetian portrait . . .[13]

> Richard Burton . . . bearded and looking like Henry VIII in a Holbein . . . caught in soft colours with a yellowish tint which suggests a Renaissance painting under old varnish: and while no particular master seems to supply the models, there is a blowzy blonde courtezan on view who has stepped straight out of a Bellini.[14]

> The film has been filtered through a sort of burnt sienna light that gives it the muted golden haze of many Renaissance paintings, and is indeed lovely to look at, but as a series of stills, not moving pictures.[15]

The tension disclosed here between pictorial 'naturalism' (designed to absorb the characters into a convincing reconstruction

[61]

of historical reality), and what might more accurately be termed a 'picturesque' style, achieved by systematic quoting of well-known visual sources (which actually draws the spectator's attention to its own patently-displayed artifice) constitutes a problem of interpretation both for this film and for Jonathan Miller's television version. The tradition of pictorial setting derives, through the intermediary of silent film, from a theatre of historical realism: its functions are ordinarily naturalistic, as exemplified by, for instance, the historical films of Luchino Visconti (e.g. *The Leopard*); and certainly by Miller's BBC *Shrew*. But there is a point at which a pictorial setting comes 'into view' in its own right, when it ceases to provide naturalistic camouflage for the figures within its frame, and becomes self-reflexive, the object of its own narcissistic gaze. Jack Jorgens feels that this style of visual design is in Zeffireli's *Shrew* so pervasive as to deprive the film of any pretensions to realism:

> Zeffirelli has little use for the realism in the play ... There are touches of vivid realistic detail in the film ... but these are used for comic effect, and work to heighten the colourful, rich portrait of Renaissance Italy. From the opening moments when Lucentio and Tranio, riding in a gentle rain, spy Padua haloed with a rainbow beyond a pastoral vision with shepherds, sheep, and greenery, the film is a beautiful idyll bathed in gold-coloured light. (Jorgens, pp. 70-1)

Tori Haring-Smith takes the argument a stage further: for her the film is not merely in appearance artificial; it is self-consciously concerned to exhibit its own artifice, and to use its picturesqueness as a framing-device capable of the same distancing effects as the play's Christopher Sly framework:

> Although he did not include Shakespeare's 'Induction', Franco Zeffirelli achieved a similar blending of reality and artificiality ... using studio realism, shading, and Panavision to keep the viewer constantly aware that the film is and is not real. Since Zeffirelli did not have the physical arrangement of a theatre to establish the metaphor of reality and illusion, he could not rely on the 'Induction' to introduce that theme. Instead, the film begins with an enormous painting of the Italian countryside. Although the picture fills the screen and the frame is not visible, the landscape is obviously unreal ... The 'real' world we view is always framed or enclosed in this way by the painted landscape.[16]

It is my view that these visual conventions do not in themselves contain clear and definitive statements of their own significance:

the meanings they make available depend largely on an interdependence with the other signifying codes of the production. Thus broadly similar design conventions, coupled with very different approaches to genre, style, and acting method, produce in Zeffirelli's film and Jonathan Miller's TV production, very dissimilar and indeed incommensurable dramatic worlds.

Within Zeffirelli's visual context of painterly composition, the principal generic emphasis is on farce. 'Zeffirelli turns the taming of Elizabeth Taylor's shrew by Richard Burton's ribald Petruchio into an assault course conducted with the comic complications of an obstacle race.'[17]

Farce is primarily of course a visual genre, depending on movement, incongruous juxtaposition, interruption, rapid reversal; and Zeffirelli makes full use of farce's principal structural motif, the chase. But farce is hardly calculated to complement or enable the careful construction of picturesque tableaux that immediately evoke the visual sources they are derived from. On the contrary, the incessant chaotic mobility of farce is likely to upset the visual stability and spatial configuration of any picturesque set. The tension between these apparently incompatible elements led critics such as David Robinson to complain about Zeffirelli's continual disturbance of the celluloid canvas:

> The first shots of Lucentio and Tranio riding out of one of those zig-zag back-drops from the Quattrocento masters and wearing, with pleasant inconsequence, clothes that seem to come from the Triumph of Maximilian, is enchanting. And the design throughout betrays a similar care. But it is largely negated by Zeffirelli's quite surprising ineptitude in composing groupings on the screen. Again and again the extravagant hurly-burlies of activity into which he launches extras and principals alike ... are as ugly as they are extravagantly busy.[18]

Other critics argued that the elaborate minutiae of naturalistic detail and the violent turbulence of rapid physical motion simply trip over one another, and reduce the visual composition to chaos:

> The intention to beguile the eye with swirling movement breaks down because so much is perpetually going on that the eventual effect is simply fussy. Dogs run about incessantly, characters hurl artefacts either to the floor or at each other; the entire cast at frequent intervals breaks into hearty communal applause or rowdy communal laughter. People fall about, or swing, Tarzan-like, on ropes; or run pointlessly after one another across roofs. After a couple of reels of this, the spectator's dearest wish is that everyone would

stand still and shut up. (Roud, *Guardian*, 3 March 1967)

The necessary reliance of farce on physical objects – doors, windows, beds, projectiles – certainly links the genre to a primarily visual, pictorial mode of presentation. Jorgens provides a brief catalogue of objects which figure in the film's physical language of 'festive destructiveness':

> Kate smashes shutters and stained-glass windows, splinters music stands and lutes, rips out the bell rope which Petruchio tugs upon so daintily, and tears loose a railing to hurl at him. Petruchio drunkenly knocks over wine glasses and pulls down curtains at Hortensio's house, smashes through railings and brick walls, and falls through the roof in Baptista's barn. He pummels and spits upon his servants, bisects a hat with a family sword causing the haberdasher to faint, tears dresses, hurls food, overturns the dinner table, and makes a shambles of the wedding bed. (Jorgens, pp. 71-2)

But these are all objects in motion, things thrown into continual kinaesthesia by the incessant physical activity of farce; they are not the scrupulously-arranged and beautifully-lit property details of a cinematic still-life portrait. Similar tendencies towards pictorial effect in Jonathan Miller's BBC production, accompanied as they are by a predominantly naturalistic approach to acting, are actually much more successful in constructing static, elaborately-framed visual compositions: with the result that the entire design concept of the production can be assimilated firmly into the nineteenth-century traditions of pictorial staging. Zeffirelli's style is much more flexible and self-deconstructing: his film with its elaborate historical and geographical setting, points even more formally towards the visual sources quoted, and yet is prepared to scatter the spatial configurations thus achieved into a turbulent mêlée of violent visual motion. No physical background, however carefully ordered and lovingly constructed, is permitted to overshadow or subdue the spontaneous physical energies of this farcical dramatic action.

An inexhaustibly inventive and subversive approach to its own formal devices is entirely in keeping with that spirit of carnival established from the outset in Zeffirelli's substituted 'Induction'. There we see the formal rituals of religion subjected to parody and inversion; and the film throughout adopts a comparably subversive perspective on the classic drama it is self-consciously mediating. The rhythms, actions, gestures and grimaces of farce continually recall Sam Taylor's 1929 (Pickford/Fairbanks) film production, the classic Hollywood 'vulgarisation' of Shakespeare; and there are even echoes of the musical *Kiss me Kate*. Some of the most obvious visual devices are parodic rather than representational in effect: reviewers unanimously noted the Burton/Henry VIII visual parallel, but traced it to its distant source in Holbein rather than to a more immediate analogue – Charles Laughton's comic portrayal of Henry VIII in Alexander Korda's *The Private Life of Henry VIII* (1933), of which Burton's performance is a direct parody. In general this self-reflexive quality of the film has up to now remained underrated or even unnoticed, though it is at certain points obvious enough – in one scene Petruchio and Grumio combine in a bawling song which actually joins in with the musical soundtrack!

It was by electing to subordinate naturalism, psychology, scholarly respect for the classical virtues and sober moral earnestness, to a sustained activation of rombustious high-jinks that Zeffirelli reaped the particular condemnation of those critics who felt that the play was being distorted, abused and wrenched from its natural or original character. The director's reliance on visual effects, whether of decor, setting or action, was felt by many observers to represent an unjustifiable sacrifice of Shakespeare's predominantly verbal dramatic medium.

> Paul Dehn, Suso Ceccho d'Amico and Zeffirelli himself, whose screenplay credit could be for dialogue reduction, skittishly recognised their debt to 'William Shakespeare, without whom they would have been at a loss for words'.
> This credit really sets the tone of the film: an indefatigable hammering playfulness which more or less assumes that no one will be paying much attention to those words they are never at a loss for.[19]

> Zeffirelli's approach to the problem . . . of understanding Shakespeare's language has seemed to be . . . to distract the audience from the words as much as possible. Sometimes you feel (wrongly I am sure) a positive contempt for the text in the lengths Zeffirelli will go to stage diversions to take your mind off it. (Robinson, *Financial Times*, 3 March 1967)

> The real trouble is, quite simply, that Shakespeare's high-spirited baby has been thrown out with the Zeffirelli bathwater.
> The director seems to have had no faith in his material, and an almost narcissistic affection for his own cleverness.
> So he has imposed chases, horseplay, slapstick, belches, false beards, carnival noses, priest-bating, crashes through walls and roofs.[20]

> ... Zeffirelli's aim seems to be to elicit fom his audience an active contempt for the words. Visual extravagance is the keynote ...²¹

> Shakespeare's text has been drastically cut, which wouldn't have been bothersome (the play is hardly one of his masterpieces) if director Franco Zeffirelli had found less oafish ways of 'opening up' the play. It seems that for most of this long movie roofs are falling in, tables of food overturning, ladies wallowing in mud. The wit and tension in the dialogues between Petruchio and Katherina are lost because Zeffirelli has them running an obstacle course while they bicker – this is to make the material cinematic, in case someone misses the point (Farber, p. 61).

I have quoted this line of hostile criticism so extensively in order to illustrate its extraordinary uniformity of tone. Such bilious reactions should be juxtaposed against Jack Jorgens's sensitive and intelligent analysis of the *purpose* and *function* of farcical business and conventions within the overall structure of the film; and with my own discussion of the complex and subtle uses of visual design. To criticise farce for being farcical is simply an absurd procedure; to contrast a version of Shakespeare unfavourably with some ideal model (which is never defined) carries very little weight as argument, and is designed only to elicit from the reader a visceral response of conformity: we don't pretend to understand the ineffable mystery of Shakespeare, but we are confident that whatever that transcendent essence may be, this isn't it. Extensive cutting of the text, the dramatisation of reported scenes such as the wedding, the substitution of visual images for verbal effects, are equally characteristic of Olivier's *Henry V*: but we would not find in commentary and criticism on that film the same accents of outraged bardolatry. Akira Kurosawa makes films of Shakespeare without using the text: they are regarded as masterpieces of cinematic interpretation.

It seems to be generally accepted that a film of Shakespeare cannot *be* 'Shakespeare': in the sense that while a theatrical performance may aspire to reactivate with some fidelity verbal and dramatic structures which were composed for a theatre, a movie has no choice but to adapt and radically interpret the material to a specifically cinematic form. It is far more productive, if that premise be accepted, to compare a film of a Shakespeare play with other film versions of Shakespeare, with other films from the repertory of the same *auteur*, with films from a comparable genre. To evaluate a film version against a conception of its 'original' is, since Shakespeare did not make films, a meaningless procedure.

IV

Both the director and those who have worked with him speak of his technique as a very free and open collaboration with the actor.

> He has a highly unselfish imagination for other people. He once said, 'You can't force an actor. He doesn't play with his technique, he plays with his own human qualities. My job is to offer many different solutions to him, and then to choose the right one. It may be comic or tragic, but it must be the right one *for him*.'[22]

> [John] Stride remembers, 'he never worked from any book. His theory was improvisation within a framework. We were never made to stick exactly to the same mode . . . Nobody wrote down the actor's moves . . . because they were never the same two nights running – there was no blocking. (quoted in Levenson, p. 92)

Yet nothing, surely, could be further from an open-ended experimental approach than the casting of Burton and Taylor as Petruchio and Katherina. Zeffirelli referred to that choice as something natural, inevitable, self-evident: 'Of course we thought of Burton and Taylor immediately' (*Evening Standard*, 5 July 1965). The Burtons, as a highly public and publicity-conscious screen couple, were in the habit of presenting to the media an image of domestic life not altogether unlike the relationship of Katherina and Petruchio. This may well have been an elaborately-constructed fantasy for media consumption, but it represents an overtly-displayed persona which blended easily into the principal roles of the *Shrew*, as it had in the previous year underpinned the laceratingly conflictual relationship in *Who's Afraid of Virginia Woolf*:

> *The Taming of the Shrew*, or the son of *Virginia Woolf*, can be best understood as cashing in on last year's success; people will apparently never tire of peeping in on a fantasy version of the Burtons' home life. (Farber, p. 61)

> Once again Elizabeth Taylor and Richard Burton clash head-on in a riot of verbal and visual fights and frolic.
> Once again they prove that theirs is certainly an explosive and often a deeply rewarding film partnership.[23]

The movie is a news event – another colourful episode in the lives

[67]

of Elizabeth Taylor and Richard Burton, whose supposed follies happen to fit into a comedy from the First Folio. Burton's Petruchio is a ringer for Henry VIII, played with broad and boozy licence. Elizabeth's Kate is a bosom heaving with feminist wiles rather than congenital bad temper. She clearly adores the brute and lets him tame her just to prolong the fun.[24]

If it is reasonable to entertain a suspicion that the principal players were cast as much for their off-screen public personalities as for their dramatic appropriateness, there would seem to be little scope for a director to promote experiment and openness. Commenting on the theatrical personalities of Burton and Taylor, Zeffirelli's philosophy of acting began to appear remarkably diluted and enfeebled:

> She's a marvellous girl. So unpredictable. She's not a set personality. You don't know everything about her and this is very exciting for a director – and it might be a problem too. You feel she has not given her best yet.
>
> Even Richard, who is a man who has done everything, has still to give his best in the movies. The best is still to come. I think they're both in progress.
>
> They're both open. I've had to be open in my own work in the past few years and always gambled. This is what we'll do with the film. There's the danger of disaster – but we'll take great pleasure in what we do. (quoted in *Evening Standard*, 5 July 1965)

Uncertain whether he is talking about Burton and Taylor or Antony and Cleopatra, Zeffirelli is here trying to make a transparent piece of type-casting sound like open-ended avant-garde experimentation.

Whether this linking of off-screen and on-screen roles was part of the director's intention or not, the massively over-exposed public personalities of the two stars inevitably coloured their participation in the film. Petruchio, for example, inherits from the Shakespearean 'Induction' the drunkenness of Christopher Sly: he appears constantly intoxicated, and at his wedding so drunk as to fall asleep during the service, waking only to gulp the communion wine with an oath. Film-viewers would not however associate the hero's drunkenness with the lost 'Induction', but with the much-publicised drunken exploits of Richard Burton, who found unlimited justification in his own cultural style – product of the Welsh mining valleys, angry young man, Bohemian artist as a young dog – for being ostentatiously drunk at every available opportunity. This aspect of the film now, after Burton's death from alcohol-related illness, evokes a mingled sense of bitter irony and lacerating pathos. Similarly, no amount of shrill vituperation, aggressive hysteria and volatile temper can disguise Elizabeth Taylor's startling physical beauty. Above all, Katherina and Petruchio are the Burton–Taylor couple – rowing and fighting, divorcing and remarrying, but always in love and always to be reunited – before they actually appear in character on the screen.

It seems therefore merely appropriate and natural that Katherina and Petruchio should, whatever their initial predispositions as mercenary fortune-hunter and mutinous virago, and in despite of the aggression and hostility enacted between them, be in love, at first sight, and in all probability happily (if noisily) ever after.

> A routine that was merely brutal – can it have even pleased its patriarchal first-night audience? – has been thawed out into a sexy light comedy. Zeffirelli is one up on the Bard by letting Petruchio and Kate fancy each other from the word go. The light of appetite, kindling in the eyes of both, suggests that the hostilities have at least some end in view. What Zeffirelli has done is to humanise Shakespeare's dreary mechanics, and turn a Punch-and-Judy show into a species of love story.[25]

The 'love-at-first-sight' motif is rendered conspicuous in the film by looks and gestures, and subsequently reinforced by Kate's silent complicity in Petruchio's announcement of their wedding, and her loyal pursuit of him to his house when he abandons her at the gates of Padua.

The 'taming' plot is thus drained of the various historical and moral significances attributed to it: its long denouement necessarily has to be translated into the terms of farce, since it has become purely a game, a mutual compact of reciprocal entertainment. Underlying the mechanical surface action we infer the presence of sexual attraction, mutual admiration and a genial and sensitive human nature. 'Richard Burton is Shakespeare's Petruchio all right: an adventurer, a self-satisfied bully, but with a touch of redeeming gaiety; and Mr Burton has a pretty moment at the end when his face betrays anxiety lest Kate should not obey his commands – and relief when she does.'[26]

These touches of 'redeeming' humanity are of course the result of actor's intervention and of directorial decision, and cannot be authenticated by reference back to Shakespeare's intentions: they are the strategies of interpretation that in all performances mediate the Elizabethan text to a contemporary audience. Elizabeth Taylor's Katherina expressed to most viewers nothing unpleasant or unattractive in her shrewishness: 'Elizabeth Taylor, her shapely bosom swelling with fury out of almost topless dresses, gives a tremendous performance as the delightful but spiteful Katherina. What a ball of fire she is, as she stands, with hands on hips, eyes blazing, leaning forward as she spits out insults like an angry swan'.[27] It is not necessary to have been insulted by a swan to recognise the accuracy of this comment: what the actress communicates is a fierce energy of sexual attraction, not a sullen force of hostile resistance.

Katherina's final speech of surrender articulates a resignation to Petruchio and to marriage; and an ironical self-consciousness calculated to suggest that the transparent accents of obedient orthodoxy belie the true vitality and sexual energy of their turbulent relationship. The first element is foregrounded by showing Kate looking in an obviously 'broody' way at some children, playing with dogs before the banquet table; and the second by displaying her immediate and passionate surrender to Petruchio's 'come kiss me, Kate'; and by having her sneak quietly out so that Petruchio has to commence the chase all over again.

Such a predominant emphasis on the central roles of the *Shrew*, with the additional reinforcement of the Burton-Taylor personality cult, inevitably left little space for any coherent or considered development of the Bianca-plot; which as many critics complained, is hardly present in the film at all.

> The film's roster of delightful performers puts up a commendable struggle against the total submersion which afflicts both plot and sub-plot.[28]

> I've no doubt that Shakespeare purists will be cross to find the Lucentio–Bianca story reduced to a sketchy outline, lots of speeches cut short and several characters missing altogether.[29]

> Zeffirelli shows himself aware that the text is still playable as it stands. His film is nearly brave, and with most of the cast he assembled, could have been tremendous: performers like Cyril Cusack (Grumio), Victor Spinetti (Hortensio, a role cut to ribbons), Michael Hordern as the shrew's father, and the young sub-plot lovers, Michael York and Natasha Pyne, could have given far more, given in turn their chance. But all is subordinated to the big, boisterous and box-office flyting of Mr Burton and Elizabeth Taylor's Kate.[30]

These comments are in no way unfair descriptions of the film's marginalisation of the Bianca-plot: a typical moment is that in which an entire scene of courtship between Lucentio and Bianca is subordinated to an extra-textual chase, Petruchio pursuing Kate around the dumbstruck lovers and out on to the rooftops. The rarified air of comic courtly love appears to stifle the boisterous energies of Petruchio and Katherina, and the film too elbows both characters and atmosphere of the sub-plot aside to escape into a more vigorous air. What little detail of the sub-plot remains in the film serves two purposes: to contrast the conventional romantic relationship of Bianca and Lucentio with the bizarre and violent wooing rituals of Petruchio and Katherina; and to juxtapose the abrasive vitality and bracing energy of Petruchio against figures of pathetic ineffectualness like Victor Spinetti's camp Hortensio, or Michael Hordern's brilliant self-parody as the synthesis of all the senescent patriarchs he has ever played.

V

By infusing the play with visual and musical overtones of romance; insisting on the reciprocal passion of tamer and tamed; translating the violence of the play into a medium of farce, where destruction is always innocuous; and by casting the end-result of these opera-tions into the form of a film, Zeffirelli has altered the rules of the game to such an extent that the film has little to say about the sexual politics of *The Taming of the Shrew*. The transformation of play into film is so complete that the historical roots of the Shakes-pearean text are scarcely any longer visible to provide the viewer with any specific structure of orientation. The sexual politics of the film can only therefore be interpreted and evaluated in terms of its own cultural context and historical moment: and I would argue that in this respect Zeffirelli's film is not so much anti-feminist as a-feminist.

Since the farce genre of the film, in its preoccupation with phys-ical capacities such as running, throwing, swinging, balancing, shouting, fighting – assumes a mutual equality and reciprocal balance of forces between the sexes, it simply does not address the questions of family and marriage in any way that would prove interesting or useful to a feminist cultural politics. Zeffirelli's ver-sion of the *Shrew* actually substitutes, for the structural antithesis of the sexes in Shakespeare's play, a new distinction: between the sterile, hypocritical and mercenary society of Padua, and the irrepressible and unassimilable energy of two Bohemian anarchists. Both Katherina and Petruchio are initially, in their different ways, at odds with conventional society; and in their fortuitous collision both find the possibility of a common cause.

> ... the 'taming' is not the heart of the film. Rather, it is the good-natured but thorough assault of Kate and Petruchio on Padua and Paduan values. Zeffirelli turns loose two rebels against hypocrites, greedy pantaloons, time-servers, blind idealists, tricky maidens, and crafty widows. They declare war on respectability, duty, religion, sighing literary romance, and narrow materialism. (Jorgens, p. 72)

Illustrations

1 & 2 (facing)
Royal Shakespeare Company production, 1960, directed by John Barton

3 & 4 (overleaf)
Royal Shakespeare Company production, 1978, directed by Michael Bogdanov

For castlists see p. 131

CHAPTER IV

Michael Bogdanov (1978)

I

Just as John Barton's production of 1960 stands at a transitional point between the inherited legacy of Stratford traditions and the challenging innovations of the new Royal Shakespeare Company so Michael Bogdanov's 1978 production of *The Taming of the Shrew* stands at a crossroads between the 'socially concerned' and wholly-state-subsidised RSC of the 1960s, with its hit musicals, Broadway transfers and substantial commercial sponsorship. Like the National Theatre, with which it shares a tangled and sometimes interdependent history, the RSC has incorporated different and even contradictory ideologies into its structural organisation and its cultural politics. The very concept of a 'national theatre' had radical origins in the nineteenth century: the first proposer of a national theatre (conceived, significantly, in the form of 'A House for Shakespeare') was a London publisher Effingham Wilson, a dissenting Whig reformer with interests in popular education. His vision was of a popular theatre which would speak directly to the people, unlike the commercial theatres of the West End.[1] The Flowers family, which was as we have seen the original begetter of the RSC, shared a similar background of political radicalism, religious free-thinking and dissent.[2] It is an axiom of modern post-structuralist cultural theory that a national theatrical institution must by definition be an ideological state apparatus, communicating and shaping a dominant culture: 'national' in the sense of a limited and exclusive concept of national ('British') culture. Yet within the historical development of both the NT and the RSC there coexists the more universal sense of 'national', a theatre which might reflect and express to the people the actuality of the nation, not in the ideal form of its Arnoldian 'best self', but in the diversity and contradictory reality of its heterogeneous experience (Elsom and Tomalin, pp. 135-47).

In the light of this contradictory history the populist and democratic credentials of the Peter Hall revolution – which we can now see clearly as more of a reform, a revitalisation of a moribund establishment by the accession to power of an energetic *petit-bourgeois* class faction – become more intelligible and even predictable. The oft-quoted radical sentiments of the RSC's leaders – 'I am a radical, and I could not work in the theatre if I were not' (Peter Hall); 'I want a socially committed theatre. A politically aware theatre' (Trevor Nunn)[3] – in addition to appearing retrospectively ironical, also identify a real historical moment in the evolution of the RSC.

As Alan Sinfield has demonstrated,[4] this early radical identity of the company consisted largely of a commitment to 'relevance' in the production of classic drama: Trevor Nunn is quoted as reporting that Peter Hall 'insisted upon one simple rule: that whenever the company did a play by Shakespeare, they should do it because the play was relevant, because the play made some demand upon our critical attention'.[5] This insistence on immediate contemporary application is, as we shall see, a fundamental principle of Michael Bogdanov's theatrical work, and a constitutive characteristic of his production of *The Taming of the Shrew*. It derives directly from a common inheritance – the enormously influential thesis of Jan Kott, whose *Shakespeare our Contemporary*[6] has probably affected twentieth-century production of Shakespeare's 'political' plays more than any other critical book. Kott's argument (which he has subsequently modified) produced a very modern version of the Shakespeare who was 'not for an age, but for all time': the paternalistic wisdom of the benevolent Victorian sage was replaced by a Shakespeare with a ruthless and unerring insight into political corruption, a formidably rational analysis of the irrationality of history, and a glimpse of the existentialist absurdity of the human condition. This was a Shakespeare who could understand fascism and totalitarianism, repression and revolution, angst and alienation – a Shakespeare whose plays could be seen as texts for the twentieth century.

Kott's argument can now be seen as in some fundamental ways a-historical. Alan Sinfield and Jonathan Dollimore[7] have demonstrated that Kott's insistence on history as an unbroken continuum of violence and exploitation is simply an inversion of the idealist conception of Tudor England as a golden age of peace and harmony. In its unitary, totalising vision Kott's thesis is as un-dialectical and a-historical as that of Tillyard. The immediate consequence of a theoretical reliance, such as that of Bogdanov, on this Marxist–existentialist philosophy is the loss of a truly materialist understanding of history, and a paradoxical endorse-ment of the universality of Shakespeare's genius: 'Shakespeare', Bogdanov insists, 'is the greatest living playwright.'[8] A theatrical enterprise which combines, in a contradictory *rapprochement*, such a respect for the authority of tradition, with a rigorous demand for contemporaneity of focus, is perhaps the ideal mixture for a theatre like the RSC. Bogdanov's radical aspirations have to be seen in the context of this phenomenon of incorporation wherein a radical appropriation of Shakespeare paradoxically serves to reinforce the cultural power of traditional authority:

> The whole business of producing Shakespeare in our society, and all the cultural authority which goes with that, depends upon the assumption that through all the metamorphoses to which the plays are subjected we still have the real presence of Shakespeare. He justifies public and private expenditure of resources and ensures the scope and quality of attention; he is the cultural token which gives significance to the interpretations which are derived from him. (Sinfield in *Political Shakespeare*, 1985, p. 174)

II

Bogdanov's use of the 'Induction' certainly represents the most inventive and exciting exploitation we will encounter of the Chris-topher Sly material: though as a number of reviewers pointed out, his idea was not original, having been used in the previous year at the Young Vic. Drawing partly on examples of Renaissance metadrama such as the audience participation of *The Knight of the Burning Pestle*, Bogdanov had his leading actor, Jonathan Pryce, join the audience, disguised as a drunk (whether Irish or Scots is among critics a matter of some dispute). Instead of introducing Christopher Sly as a stage character and as the butt of trickery and practical jokes of which the audience is aware, this production set out to trick its audience: by staging, ~~in the manner of Augusto Boal's 'invisible theatre'~~, an incident in the auditorium itself between the apparent drunk and an apparent usherette (who was actually Paola Dionisotti, the actress playing Katherina). Calculated to be oblivious to this dissimilation, the audience was distracted and disturbed by a noisy and violent altercation, in which Pryce/Sly/Petruchio insisted rudely on his rights against attempts by Dionisotti/Hostess/Katherina to control and suppress him – an effective adaptation of the opening scene of *The Shrew*. The ostensible spontaneity of this incident was actually carefully scripted:

> SLY: Jim. It's all right, my mate's got my ticket. What's the matter with you? It's no problem, all right? Jim! Heh! It's all right, there's no problem. I'm not making an exhibition of myself, what's the matter with you? 'Don't cry for me, Argentina!' Look it's all right, there's no problem.
>
> You've done what? what have you done? You've sent for the police, have you? All right, you get the police, I'll wait here. Don't you bloody well talk to me like that, I've got every right to be in here. If there's anybody going to get sorted out around here, it's you, all right? You're not going to talk to me like that. All right, I'll wait right here, OK? You can't tell me what to do – no bloody woman's going to tell me what to do.
>
> I'll wait here, OK? If there's anybody going to get sorted out it's you. OK, I'll wait here, go on, you go and get the police.
>
> What's your game, chief? What's the matter with you? Look I've got no argument with you, it's just her. Don't you talk to me like that, you bloody cow. Look, leave it out will you?[9]

By means of this brilliant *coup de théâtre*, Bogdanov produced his Christopher Sly directly out of an (apparently) real-life context of coarse violence and brutal masculinity: some members of the audience were, according to Bernard Levin, so completely taken in that they rose to call the police.

The truly *dramatised* nature of the event soon became apparent, however, as the anonymous drunk clambered on to the stage and proceeded to demolish the set. The stage had been deliberately decorated with an old-fashioned period set, all too familiar to those with longer memories of Stratford productions, but quite out of keeping with RSC style in the late seventies. Red plush proscenium curtains framed an almost operatic Italianate scene, with arches and fountains, painted flats, 'plywood pilasters, wobbly loggias, a perspective street scene framing a beefy classical statue'.[10] As Jonathan Pryce vandalised these apparent preparations for an 'ultra-traditional' production, devastating the set and dragging down the red drapes to reveal a much more contemporary stage structure of scaffolding and metallic catwalks, the dramatic nature of his intervention began to reveal itself. Christopher Sly had been assigned the task of preparing a contemporary audience for a production of acute contemporary relevance and application: by towing the coarse language of the streets with him into the charmed circle of the Shakespearean stage; by foregrounding, in the form of his encounter with the usherette, immediate and everyday questions of masculine domination and female subordination; and by destroying, in a potently visible and overtly metadramatic gesture, the familiar properties of traditional Shakespeare production.

The most likely effect of such an opening, which adapted the Shakespearean 'Induction' to construct an expose of theatrical illusion itself, would be analogous to Brechtian 'alienation': we would expect the audience to be aroused and sensitised into an alert and vigilant awareness of the constructed and artificial nature of the entire presentation. That was not however entirely or even primarily Michael Bogdanov's intention: he had no wish to establish a Brechtian relationship between performance and reality:

> I don't really believe in Brecht's 'alienation'. I don't believe you can objectify the theatrical experience in the way that Brecht intended. Therefore I do try to draw the audience into the experience emotionally, and then shock them. I suppose that is alienation in that respect; lulling them into that false sense of security, then disrupting it.[11]

The director seems to have been much more concerned to create a theatrical environment of complete empathy on the part of the spectator: an emotional absorption perhaps more akin to Piscator's 'total theatre' than to Brecht's *Verfremdungseffekt*.

> The act of theatre was self-reflexive, but leaving the nerve ends raw and tingling, ready for the violent experience to come. The violence of my production was meant to engage the audience on an emotional level, to the extent of asking the audience to sit up and be counted. To ask what do you really believe, are you really sitting comfortably in your seats, or is there something else that theatre makes you do? Makes you angry, makes you fear, challenges you, and finally makes you want to do something to change the world. Catharsis has no meaning for me. I'm not interested in people purging their emotions

[77]

in the theatre and then walking away without a care in the world. I am only interested in theatre that excites people enough to make them want to cheer, or be angry enough to walk out. (pp. 91-2)

In practice, the challenge to conventional notions of precisely where the borderline between everyday reality and theatrical illusion should be drawn, was more extensive and more radical than the director's own remarks suggest. Several reviewers seem to have been excited by the proceedings of the reconstructed induction to such an extent that they failed to attend with apropriate vigilance to the carefully modulated transitions by means of which the production shifted into a more recognisably Shakespearean discourse. Robert Cushman felt that the transition was abrupt and inexplicable:

> Enter, as in Shakespeare's Induction, a Lord, who proposes to dress Sly up as an another Lord . . . then, though no players have been announced, *The Taming of the Shrew* starts; Mr Pryce is (a) bemused, (b) embroiled, (c) Petruchio. The show is now plainly his dream, but at what point it began – or why, before the play proper, he should talk modern and everyone else Elizabethan, I couldn't say.[12]

Irving Wardle of *The Times* commented in similar vein: 'The main justification for all this is that it gives Jonathan Pryce the chance to play both Sly and Petruchio. As he disappears into the second role, never to reappear in the first, the pattern does not make much sense, but who cares . . .' (*The Times*, 5 May 1978). It was certainly the director's intention to substitute for the Renaissance device of the commissioned private performance by travelling players, a view of the play as 'Sly's dream':

> Sly, the drunken tinker is thrown out of the pub by the hostess, falls asleep, and dreams a dream of revenge and power; not only power over women, but class power through wealth. The first image that comes to him in his dream is the huntsman who bets on the dog in exactly the same way, and with the same amounts of money, as the women are bet on at the end of the play. (Bogdanov in *The Shakespeare Myth*, 1988, pp. 90-1)

Sly is certainly asleep before the Lord enters: though whether the dream convention was invoked with sufficient clarity remains a matter of dispute: activity on stage, unless extremely stylised, tends to declare an independent life of its own, rather than admit a tenuous existence as the figment of a sleeping character's imagination. Nonetheless, the inevitable movement towards Shakespeare was actually engineered gradually and with considerable skill. The rest of Shakespeare's 'Induction', scene i was played through complete, but with Sly sustained in his modern persona, so that the Renaissance dialogue of the Lord and his huntsmen was allowed to establish a powerful contrast with the demotic idiom of Christopher Sly's intervention. As 'Induction' scene ii opened, with Sly revealed in a bathtub being 'scrubbed by a gang of deferential heavies' (Wardle, *The Times*, 5 May 1978), the colloquial accents of modernity reappeared, now thrown into a polyphonic altercation with the inherited Shakespearean discourse:

> SLY: Hey, what's going on? hey, what's happening? What are you doing? Hey lads, look, listen, get off, will you? get off! Look, I was just having a quiet drink, honest lads, I wasn't doing anything. Look, get us a pint of bitter, would you, chief? Argh, that's cold. What are you doing? What's your game, chief? Hey, look, get us a pint of bitter, would you, yeh, one of you? look, what's going on? I was just having a quiet drink, honest I was.
> I could get to like this.
> LORD: Will't please your lordship drink a cup of sack?
> SLY: Lordship? What are you talking about? My name's Sly – Christopher Sly – and I've never drunk sack in my life. Just get me a pint of bitter, would you?
> SERVANT: What raiment will your honour wear today?

When Sly's ramblings eventually make contact with the Shakespearean text, it is in a ruthlessly modernised form:

> SERVANT: Heaven cease this idle humour in your honour!
>   O that a mighty man of such descent
>   Should be infused with so foul a spirit!
> SLY: You what? Are you trying to make me mad? Are you trying to tell me I'm not Christopher Sly, old Sly's son of Walton Vale, born a tinker and now by present profession unemployed? You ask Fat Marion, the barmaid at the Engineer's, if she doesn't know me.

Ultimately however the deceptive strategies of the Lord are powerful enough to transform Sly's earthy contemporary patois into the mellifluous cadences of Elizabethan blank verse:

> Am I a lord, and I've got such a lady?
> Or do I dream? or have I dreamed till now?

Clearly the principal feature of this production's visual design lay in the abrupt contrast between the acquiescent traditionalism of the false set, and the spare, insistent modernity of the real one. The conventional pictorial set was established to signify a number of things: the preoccupation with a remote historical past characteristic of many productions of this play (e.g. both the Zeffirelli and Miller versions); the aesthetics of naturalism, which invests its reductive meanings in the transparent simulation of real houses, streets, palaces; and above all the entire repertory of physical properties associated with conventional Shakespearean production – the prompt-book stipulates that one of the objects to be pulled down by Sly is a *'Romeo and Juliet* balcony'. In a graphically unmistakable visual language the 'Induction' declared Bogdanov's directorial intentions: to reject the academic historicism of other producers; to disrupt the legacy of nineteenth-century pictorial realism; and to provoke an iconoclastic resistance to the dominance of convention in the contemporary production of Shakespeare. Whatever opportunities may have been afforded to the actors in this obviously spectacular and exciting *coup de théâtre*, its primary function was to formulate in concrete and visible terms the director's theatrical vision.

The set proper was much more in keeping with the RSC's current 'house-style' as well as with Bogdanov's personal preoccupations: both clamorously modern and refreshingly open after the confined spaces of the traditional set.

> (Sly) tore apart all the illusory scenery, revealing a respectably contemporary series of rusty metal frames, staircases, and cat-walks.

> Chris Dyer's set, an elaborate structure of rusting iron arches, suggests a combination of the west wing at San Quentin and Paddington Station.[13]

> (Sly) demolishes Chris Dyer's set to a smoking ruin, dumping spectators back in the usual open spaces of this company's house style. (Wardle, *The Times*, 5 May 1978)

It is apparent from these comments, and from the evolution of RSC style through the sixties and seventies, that the theatrical inversion of Bogdanov's 'Induction' certainly shocked and disrupted audience sensibilities in terms of habitual theatrical expectations. But in terms of visual style, the inversion operated in the opposite direction, overthrowing what was already, to experienced members of the audience, old-fashioned, stilted and unfamiliar; and substituting in its place a more 'usual', 'respectably contemporary' medium of stage design. Only the most reactionary of critics, such as B. A. Young writing in the *Financial Times*, found the genuine set 'unrepresentative'.[14] Given the probable composition of a Stratford main-house audience, with its social, cultural and educational range – from the casual visitor to the enlightened theatre-goer, from the innocent tourist to the hardened press reviewer, from the conscripted attendance of a school pupil to the voluntary participation of a genuine devotee – the inversion of visual discourse is likely to have provoked reactions from outrage to bewilderment to a gratified pleasure at the restoration of contemporary theatrical fashions. Within the new conventions of a modernist style, the 'constructivist' set performed a double function: that of welding the play indissolubly to the spectator's contemporary experience; and that of wresting it from the stylistic inheritance of romantic and farcical 'period' appropriations, the decorative and colourful pageantry of the past, in order to deliver it over to the harsh metallic outlines of a bleak and inhospitable social environment. No visual splendours of Renaissance costume and architecture were there to soften cruelty and oppression into high-spirited tussling or philanthropic solicitude: in the impersonal outlines of this industrial frame, the battle of the sexes could become a hard and brutal affair.

Modernity of stage design was complemented by modernity of costume. Bogdanov favours modern dress as the standard uniform for classic plays, since his purpose in adapting them is to highlight their ostensible parallels with our own contemporary world.

> There is no question of treating the plays as archaic anachronisms: you have to relate them to the society in which you live in order to make immediate contact with the audience. If that contact is made by presenting the plays in a particular way, then that is the way to do them. I work in modern dress all the time, because I find that method erects the least barriers between the audience and the language of the plays. There are other directors, of course, who are very successful in working in other ways. But I find that modern dress is the method I need to employ to highlight the contemporary parallels.
> (Bogdanov in *The Shakespeare Myth*, 1988, p. 92)

In pursuit of those contemporary parallels, as we have seen,

Bogdanov was concerned to stress the continuities between the mercantile ethics of Renaissance Padua and the commercial values of modern-day British capitalism; between the oppression of women in Shakespeare's time, and the continuing exploitation of the sex today; between the class-divisions of the sixteenth century and the economic inequality of the twentieth.

Towards this ultimate super-objective, the resources of contemporary costume were drawn upon in an eclectic variety of ways. As the scruffy drunk from the auditorium collapsed centre-stage into an intoxicated stupor, the Lord and his huntsmen made a spectacular entrance dressed in traditional 'hunting pink': the visual language of costume overtly confronting the immediate realities of class and economic injustice: 'The lights . . . rose to reveal the Lord and his huntsmen in sinister outline, smoothly complacent in modern red hunting outfits' (Warren, p. 201). A bloody fox's pelt was slung contemptuously over the recumbent Sly, thus underlining his status as victim. The hunting motif became a pervasive metaphor throughout the production, symbolising first the exploitation of Sly, and then the subjection of women: Bogdanov saw the betting sequence in the final scene, where men wager on the performance of their wives, as the fulfilment of a recurrent pattern of mastery and victimisation encapsulated in the metaphor of the hunt. Thus the baying of hounds and the winding of hunting horns accompanied the end as well as the beginning of the play.

The persistent emphasis of the modern costume (see illustration 3), which had a distinctively Italianate flavour, was on a visual definition of the monied section of a commercialised society. 'The Lord became Baptista, a wealthy tycoon surrounded by servants in impeccably cut morning suits . . .'(Warren, p. 201). Economic relationships were stressed by pushing the parallels with modern cultural and commercial relationships: 'Padua is a fashionable and pretentious arts centre, while a sharp Italianate sophistication floods over Chris Dyer's cool grey and brown set like a freshly spilt Martini. Petruchio straddles a motor-bike, Katherina and Bianca bear the finished perfection of a Ferregamo window display, while their father tots up their suitors' assets on a business calculator.'[15] Many critics sensed a certain gimmickry in the use of props like the motor-bike for Petruchio's horse, or Baptista's calculator; and the multiplication of farcical business around the contrast between the inherited Shakespearean legacy and the details of modern

[82]

experience. One called the production a failed attempt at the 'High Camp' style of Shakespearean performance. But there can be no doubt that the principal motivations underlying the modernity of style and design were moral and political preoccupations.

The final banquet was staged around a green baize gaming table, the male guests supplied with brandy and cigars, the ambience of exclusively masculine preserves like clubs and gambling houses (see illustration 4). The smoky atmosphere of male freemasonry and society sport was deemed the appropriate environment for a conclusive demonstration of masculine power over women. The general effect was described particularly well by Benedict Nightingale in the *New Statesman*:

> Padua, it seems, is that sort of place, a competitive, grasping, cynical, and really rather horrible city. A city in which well-fed men slouch indolently over their port, baying 'hear, hear' when one of their number extracts a particularly ignominious confession of inferiority from his woman. A city where the sound of the hunting-horn echoes symbolically over the walls. A city in which a man as unscrupulous and deadly as Jonathan Pryce's Petruchio is all too sure to thrive.[16]

IV

The principal emphasis in the acting style of the leading players was on violence. For Bogdanov the quality of personal relationships always expresses in immediate and concrete form the nature of a society. The abuses and structural injustices of a competitive, individualistic economy can be mirrored in the violent physical encounters of its members: the predatory commercialism of the Paduan business community may be symbolised by the exploitative confrontations of its citizens.

Katherina and Petruchio thus enacted their microcosmic class-struggle in an atmosphere of violent physical struggle and abuse. 'The production made no attempt to soften the brutality of Petruchio's methods; the first scene with Kate was a violent physical struggle, not a wit-combat' (Warren, p. 201). The role of Petruchio was played in an almost literal endorsement of his manservant's allegations of 'madness':

> Hazlitt advised all husbands to study the character of Petruchio but Bogdanov turns him into a psychopath. The soliloquy in Act 2, scene

1 in which he declares how sweetly he will woo the notorious Kate is spoken while he twists a white silk scarf in what could be murderous hands.[17]

Jonathan Pryce, graduating from Sly to Petruchio, transforms him into a manic chauvinist pig (Billington, *Guardian*, 5 May 1978).

The power of Jonathan Pryce's acting to communicate menace, threat, a disturbing potentiality for violence, was perceived by most critics in exactly the way Bogdanov intended it should be: as a disclosure of the true brutality in Shakespeare's text, exposed in order to render it emotionally repulsive and morally opprobrious.

It is Petruchio who repels us with his inhumanity, passionate for his quarry's wealth, dispassionate towards suffering. With frightening speed he switches from hysterical bouts of clowning to dark, brutish rages which give his boast to 'kill a wife with kindness' a psychopathic horror. (Ellison, *Evening Standard*, 5 May 1978)

Direct physical violence comes almost as a relief in the work of this alarming actor; what really rivets the tension is the fear of what he may do next. You know that he is confined within the role, which he delivers with fine, snarling precision, but you can never tell where those reptilian movements and spasms of murderous energy are going to stop. 'He that knows better how to tame a shrew, now let him speak. Eh?' he says, raking us with a derisive gaze, and then turning on his heel, stuffing a bottle in his pocket. (Wardle, *The Times*, 5 May 1978)

Faced with a sustained campaign of attempted subordination at the hands of such a man, Katherina clearly faces a stark choice, of submission or resistance. There is no 'love at first sight' here: on the contrary, 'there was certainly no hint of possible relationship, much less affection, between her and Petruchio' (Warren, p. 202). Paola Dionisotti played Katherina as a forceful and assertive woman, who resists the power of masculine domination with all the resources at her command, and ultimately denies Petruchio the satisfaction of achieved and assured control. Her undefeated resistance became apparent, for some observers, in the final scene: where in making her formal speech of submission (see illustration 4), Dionisotti conveyed a sense of withheld loyalty, by inserting an ironical distance between the subjected person and her public declaration of complicity.

Paola Dionisotti's somewhat stunned Kate discovers a breathtakingly sarcastic poise that isn't very far from scorn in her public submission to her husband's orders.[18]

Katherina [is Petruchio's] match in spleen and forbidding looks; but not entirely entering into the role of victim. It is unclear at which moment she begins to crack, and there is an element of personal irony in the final submission foreign to a game of unconditional surrender (Wardle, *The Times*, 5 May 1978).

Other observers felt that Katherina's resistance was sustained by a kind of dumb insolence, taking the terms of her subordination with such literalness that they were rendered ludicrous and therefore questionable: 'Miss Dionisotti gets round her big repentance speech partly by personalising it (as both her husband and her playright instruct her) but most of all by taking it literally. When she says she will put her hand beneath her husband's foot, she does so – and he, moved and a little appalled, withdraws the foot' (Cushman, *Observer*, 7 May 1978).

Thus far we have encountered a style of acting which perfectly complements the director's moral, political and theatrical intentions: a performance medium which renders the taming story as a fable of masculine oppression and female subordination, and exposes the play's latent content of cruelty and brutalisation. The emphases on intense physicality and on violence are however rather more problematical than these accounts by themselves suggest. It has become apparent in recent debates around issues like rape and violence against women, that representations of physical assault performed on victimised women by aggressively masculine men cannot simply be assumed to guarantee an acceptable moral response. The kinds of theatrical excitement generated by such representations appear to be somewhat more double-edged, and the strategy of mobilising such violence between actors to be a more dangerous procedure than Bogdanov's straightforward ethical feminism would imply. It would certainly appear to me that his lack of interest in techniques of distancing and alienation, his commitment to the excitements of an intensely experiential theatre, would be likely to impose little moral or intellectual restraint on the release of emotions of which the director's politico–moral perspective would scarcely approve. Nothing could have been further from Bogdanov's intentions than to suggest that Katherina is as much a masochist as Petruchio is a sadist: but that reading of the producion seems to have been available to some observers: 'Paola Dionisotti's Kate is a hard-faced bitch with a strident voice, a mean temper and, hidden somewhere beneath, the masochism to relish Petruchio's more imaginative outrages' (Nightingale, *New Statesman*, 12 May 1978). To hold Bogdanov and his actors responsible for this alarming deployment of the vocabulary of sexist abuse would perhaps be an overstatement. But some of the excitements offered by the acting seem to me at least to contain some dangerous potentialities. Benedict Nightingale's celebration of the emotional intensity of the performance compares rather disturbingly with Michael Bogdanov's comments, quoted earlier, on the desirability of charging an audience with acute emotional excitement:

> This is a terrific performance, packed with anger and aggro, and by no means lacking in finesse. Notice the triumphant little wriggle of the tamer's shoulders when his animal first submits, or the secret clenching and stretching of his fist when he tests her obedience in Baptista's circus-ring . . . As I watched him at work, a rabbit to his snake, I began to wonder if we hadn't all become a little too satisfied with the company's acknowledged virtues, its coldness and sophistication, its feeling for irony and itch for complexity, its knack for giving five or six simultaneous meanings to one flattish line. Hasn't it become excessively chary of the glands and the gut, the stomach and the smoking bowels? (Nightingale, *New Statesman*, 12 May 1978).

The Bianca-plot was thoroughly integrated into this production, though no use at all was made of its potentialities for developing and foregrounding the themes of illusion, deception, dissimulation and disguise. Since Jonathan Pryce doubled as Sly and Petruchio, there was no onstage audience to encourage and sustain any doubleness of perspective or metadramatic awareness: Sly disappeared completely until the closing moments when another actor impersonated him observing the final scene; and with Sly went the play's capacity for self-reflexive theatrical discourse. The sub-plot action was therefore made to serve the main 'taming' plot, rather than being permitted to develop its own emphases on romantic courtship, comic wooing, deception of self and of others.

Bogdanov found the sub-plot useful chiefly as a means to evoking a general social condition rather than an isolated individual case. The mercenary and commercial priorities of Padua, the universal competition for wealth and status, the buying and selling of the female body, were revealed more forcefully as endemic to a particular social structure. Petruchio's assertion of the profit-motive

('I come to wive it wealthily in Padua') met with no surprise or resistance from Baptista, who appeared if anything impressed with his prospective son-in-law's commercial instincts. Having disposed of the obstructive shrew, the merchant immediately proceeded to auction off his younger daughter. Bogdanov exaggerated and insisted on the mercenary squalor of this human meat-market: Baptista sat at a huge gilt desk, adding up the relative values of the suitors' offers on an automatic calculator. When one offer incorporated land and agricultural stock, the city merchant had to check a digest of farm-prices to ascertain the real value of this particular applicant for his daughter's hand.

The production used modern dress throughout (see illustration 3) in order to emphasise the immediate contemporary relevance and applicability of the play's preoccupations, its themes of class and money, abuse and exploitation. This detailed emphasis on money and profit persisted throughout: its final image was of Petruchio's servant Grumio clambering across a table to retrieve the wager earned for his master by Katherina's compliance. Petruchio exited with Kate in one hand, and a cheque ostentatiously written by Baptista as an additional dowry (or rather a bonus for the success of his 'taming') in the other. Bianca herself occupied a secure niche in this competitive world: poised and beautiful, she showed herself (see illustration 4) as contemptuous of her sister as of her unwanted suitors.

> Bianca, usually the play's romantic nub, is played by Zoe Wanamaker as a spoiled minx, capable of cackling derisively at a lovelorn admirer. If the younger sister is superficially more agreeable, it's because she has been more successful in the running contest for the status of father's pet. Her venomous, flouncing exit after Baptista shifts his approval, followed by Katherina's slightly dazed one, suggests that the two of them have ended by swapping roles and that from now on Bianca will be the shrew. (Nightingale, *New Statesman*, 12 May 1978)

V

The most striking and radical contrast of interpretation we will encounter in this study lies between Jonathan Miller's production for BBC television, discussed in the next chapter, and Michael Bogdanov's RSC version. Miller's production is based on a form of academic historicism, overtly moralising and even religious, studiously avoiding contemporary ideological problems, committed to decoding the 'taming' story as the fable of a companionate marriage disciplined by the ideal of the ordered family. Bogdanov's was explicitly socialist and feminist, a sustained assault on capitalist values and on the subordination of women. Yet curiously both directors have claimed that their respective productions were based on a serious attempt to understand the play *historically*.

The intellectual horizons of Bogdanov's production were constituted by Marxist historical theory, contemporary feminism and Freudian psychoanalysis. Like all Bogdanov's work in the theatre, this production was rooted in Jan Kott's influential conception of Shakespeare as 'our contemporary': and Bogdanov further believes firmly that Shakespeare's own views were progressive and feminist. The play in his view attempts an exposure of mercenary relationships and of the unjust subordination of women; which in the production was accomplished partly by foregrounding the 'Induction', which the director sees as theoretically and dramatically essential to the play's meaning. The 'taming' story becomes Christopher Sly's fantasy of getting even with the Hostess who evicts him from the pub: the play is 'a wish-fulfilment dream of a male for revenge on a female' (Bogdanov in *The Shakespeare Myth*, 1988, p. 90). A modern production should, however, challenge this patriarchal fantasy by showing 'Petruchio chastened and Kate victorious'.[19] Kate's final speech of submission in this production was not delivered either as a voluntary acceptance of marital subordination, or as the public façade of a private intimacy, but rather as the enforced compliance of an imposed servitude. The historical character of both play and production thus depend for Bogdanov on a sense of historical continuity: the predatory, commercialised world of Shakespeare's Padua can be linked directly to contemporary experience; the feminist vision of the progressive Elizabethan dramatist transcends history to meet and embrace the feminism of the modern socialist director. Here is Bogdanov's own summary of his views on the play:

> No play is written outside the social context that conditions the behaviour of its characters. *The Taming of the Shrew* has traditionally been seen as a play supporting the male view of the world. To many it is repugnant. Charles Marowitz in a brutal, truncated version took the themes to their logical extremes. The debate as to whether Kate

or Petruchio has won will go on forever, but look for the clues outside their relationship. Examine the few lines of Christopher Sly, the drunken tinker and his battle with 'the woman of the house': his revenge dream of taming the shrew. How do the other women in the play respond to the bet in the final scene? Why is Katherina's speech of submission so embarrassingly long? What is the importance of the huntsmen in the induction and of so many hunting images? In this world where bodies are sold to the highest bidder Kate's attempt to establish independence challenges the regime and the preconceived ideas of a woman's role in society. Does Shakespeare *really* believe that this is the way that society should behave or is he asking for an egalitarian society of equal rights and opportunities? (Bogdanov, *Shakespeare Lives!*, p. 5)

Michael Bogdanov's general approach to the revival of Shakespearean drama is, in line with one significant trend in the RSC's contradictory ideology, to appropriate it for a politically-committed socialist application to immediate contemporary issues and problems. In order to secure this effect of urgent contemporary relevance it is not necessary, in Bogdanov's view, to wrest the plays from their original and intrinsic meanings: since the essence of their contemporary relevance consists in the fact that they successfully analysed and indicted the capitalism of an earlier period, and can thus be pointed, with no distortion or falsification of their essential spirit, at the injustice and exploitation endemic to a later stage of the same economic and political system.

> I don't see any point in directing Shakespeare for the stage unless you treat him, as Jan Kott described him, as 'our contemporary' . . . Some things that Shakespeare wrote about were intensely parochial and local, and other themes, particularly his major themes – the nature of power and the territorial imperative – are things that pertain today, just as much as they did four hundred years ago. In what was a pre-capitalist era, he analysed that era in a way that is relevant to the capitalism of today. The nature of kingship and power is exactly the same now as it was then. (Bogdanov in *The Shakespeare Myth*, 1988, p. 92)

This view of history as an unbroken continuum of violence and exploitation links, in a transhistorical dimension, the humanity as well as the injustice of the present with those of the past. Just as there is no radical break in the historical evolution of modern society from its Renaissance origins, so the liberal and enlightened wisdom imputed to a modern socialist intellectual can be located in the ideology of an Elizabethan dramatist; Shakespeare's plays offer a continual endorsement of the values of contemporary

[89]

democratic socialism:

> He is, all the time, analysing the nature of power and the way that
> it corrupts man. It is as if he were trying to find another society that
> could exist outside of this Elizabethan one of greed and avarice . . .
> I believe that Shakespeare implies that individual action is always
> doomed to failure, and collective action is probably the only way to
> right the wrongs of this society. (p. 94)

In sharp contradistinction to Jonathan Miller's sense of the radical
discontinuity between Renaissance and modern views on
marriage, the family, the nature of women, Bogdanov believes that
Shakespeare held, in relation to the Tudor era, views on these
matters that are easily assimilable to contemporary feminist
thought.

> I believe Shakespeare was a feminist, and all the plays I direct
> analyse the roles of women from that ideological point of view . . .
> (he) shows women totally abused – like animals – bartered to the
> highest bidder. He shows women used as commodities, not allowed
> to choose for themselves. In *The Taming of the Shrew* you get that
> extraordinary scene between Baptista, Grumio and Tranio, where
> they are vying with each other to see who can offer most for Bianca,
> who is described as 'the prize'. It is a toss of the coin to see which
> way she will go: to the old man with a certain amount of money, or
> to the young man, who is boasting that he's got so many ships. She
> could end up with the impotent old fool, or the young 'eligible' man:
> what sort of life is that to look forward to? There is no question of
> it, his sympathy is with the women, and his purpose, to expose the
> cruelty of a society that allows these things to happen. (p. 89)

The immanent structure of the play itself thus guarantees, if
appropriately and correctly adapted, a feminist perspective on its
own contents. Though in principle Bogdanov believes in uncon-
strained liberty of interpretation, he sees the *Shrew* as a play which
contains, encoded in its intrinsic and organic structure, the
ideological resources necessary for the delivery of feminist ideas.
To an interviewer's suggestion that the play might be considered
to reflect the misogynistic thought of its age, and to possess the
value of a historical document rather than to represent a source
of enlightened liberal opinion, Bogdanov replied:

> Everybody is entitled to their own subjective view of the play, and
> in that sense, you could play it as a sexist drama. But you would
> have to cut something out; that is my point, you must distort some
> of the lines, or be called to account for what they mean. To play it
> as a sexist piece you would have to cut the 'Induction' for it is in

that scene that the clues to the play's real nature are set down . . . You can only see it as a sexist play if you misunderstand what Shakespeare has actually written. (p. 91)

VI

Earlier in this chapter (see above, p. 88) I quoted Bogdanov's allusion to Charles Marowitz's 'brutal, truncated version' of *The Taming of the Shrew*, which took the themes of male supremacy and female subordination 'to their logical extremes'. Bogdanov was conscious of adopting a very different approach: where Marowitz saw the play in its 'classic' formation as essentially 're-pugnant', Bogdanov believes its true meaning is compatible with modern feminist ideology: 'Bogdanov's Shakespeare is sitting somewhere apart with you, me and the other right-thinking people, boggling at the cruelty and crudity of it all' (Nightingale, *New Statesman*, 12 May 1978). Marowitz's *'collage'* version, *The Shrew*, presents a useful and interesting comparison with Bogdanov's production, since it constitutes a parallel project of 'modernisation' attempted and accomplished from a completely different viewpoint and by completely different means; and since it represents some of the bolder avant-garde experimentation that could be undertaken outside dominant theatrical institutions like the RSC, in the financially impoverished but theoretically daring world of 'alternative' theatre.

Most of the critical reactions to Bogdanov's production commended his discovery of modern liberal ideas in Shakespeare's text; some critics on the other hand felt that the production's devastating disclosure of the play's brutality and cruelty rendered it so offensive to a modern audience that it should no longer be revived at all. Notwithstanding Bogdanov's conviction of the progressive nature of the *Shrew*'s sexual politics, some observers felt that the play had become temperamentally unsuitable to the modern age:

> What we cannot ignore for long is . . . the distasteful nature of the theme.(Shorter, *Daily Telegraph*, 1 May 1979)

> There is, however, a larger question at stake than the merits or otherwise of this particular production. It is whether there is any reason to revive a play that seems totally offensive to our age and our society. My own feeling is that it should be put back firmly and squarely on the shelf, (Billington, *Guardian*, 5 May 1979)

This spirit of moral and intellectual hostility towards the original play was Marowitz's starting-point. His several 'collage' versions of Shakespeare's plays, developed in his own 'fringe' theatre the Open Space, tackled the problems of modern reception by adopting a radically avant-garde freedom with the texts, reconstructing them by cutting, transposing, de- and re- contextualising. He described his own version of *Hamlet* as 'spliced-up into a collage with lines juxtaposed, sequences re-arranged, characters dropped or blended, and the entire thing played out in short, discontinuous fragments which appeared like subliminal flashes out of Hamlet's life and, in every case, used Shakespeare's words, though radically re-arranged'[20] *The Shrew* (1973) went further in re-contextualisation by interposing between sections of the reconstructed Shakespeare material a series of scenes featuring a modern 'Boy and Girl', designed to represent contemporary versions of Hortensio and Bianca. The sustained parallel of past and present actions was intended as a means of securing a constant double focus, and of promoting a continual awareness of the remoteness and difference of the original Shakespeare play. In practice the parallel scenes, as Marowitz himself recognised, remained despite protracted reworking theatrically weak and ideologically pointless.[21] The reconstructed Shakespeare plot, however, remains a powerful attempt to challenge and subvert the patriarchal ideology contained within the structure of the old play.

Marowitz's general intention was to 'convert Shakespeare's comedy into a Gothic tragedy . . . Shakespeare's combative couple had to leave the realms of farce and transmute themselves into a kind of Grimm fairy-tale world of sinister archetypes and hopeless victims' (*Marowitz Shakespeare*, pp. 17-18). The focus on physical violence which characterised Bogdanov's subsequent production was in Marowitz's adaptation taken much further, with a continual emphasis on cruelty and brutality, malice and aggression. There were scenes of torture, and a particularly brutal and deliberately offensive scene in which Petruchio forces Katherina to submit to anal rape.

Marowitz saw Petruchio as 'a kind of Mafiosa-monster who still covets Baptista's fortune and is fully prepared to instigate a bloodless courtship to obtain it'; 'a man whose peculiar psychosis insists on total subservience as the emblem of love', and is 'motivated even more strongly by the detestable spirit of independence that throbs inside of Katherina' (*Marowitz Shakespeare*, p. 18). All comedy was abolished as Petruchio's campaign of extortion, exploitation and oppression was played out as a series of violent encounters of will: between Katherina and Bianca, Petruchio and Baptista, Petruchio and Katherina. The text becomes full of images of imprisonment, confinement, torture – all derived from the Shakespeare text, but thrown into sharper relief by the discontinuous fragmenting effects of the collage technique, and connecting much more readily with the cultural and historical landscape of the early 1970s. The physical and mental cruelty of the 'taming' process was conceived as a process of 'brainwashing': in a highly ritualised wedding-scene, Kate was handled into a bridal gown 'like a mechanical doll'. At Petruchio's house she was tortured by deprivation of food, sleep and sensory reassurance. This penultimate scene ends with Kate resisting Petruchio's sexual approaches using lines spoken to Christopher Sly by the Page in Shakespeare's 'Induction', scene ii: 'Pardon me yet for a night or two . . .' Petruchio's response to this plea for consideration is to have his servants pinion Katherina across a table while he inflicts on her a violent and degrading act of 'buggery'.

The final scene was transformed from a family dinner at Baptista's house to a Kafkaesque trial scene:

> Lights up on a surreal tribunal-setting. PETRUCHIO sits behind a high tribunal-desk. He is looking straight ahead. In the background, there is the unmistakable murmur of womens' voices; chatting, gossiping, conniving. After a moment GRUMIO, dressed in a black gown like an official of the Court, bangs his staff three times. The whispering stops.
> KATE is ushered in by BAPTISTA. She is wearing a simple, shapeless institutional-like garment. She stares straight ahead and gives the impression of being mesmerized. Her face is white; her hair drawn back; her eyes wide and blank.

Kate delivered her speech of submission mechanically, by rote, 'as if the words were being spoken by another'. Hesitating between complete passivity and hysterical resistance, Kate was constantly prompted and prodded by husband and father to speak out her manifesto of abjection. The production closed with the image of the modern Boy and Girl posing for a wedding photograph, superimposed on this powerful tableau of female subordination.

There is little in the text to suggest that Katherina endures anything other than utter defeat, imprisoned and institutionalised, brainwashed and mesmerised, her resistance broken and her spirit quelled. This was not at all, however, the effect of the production. The *Guardian*'s critic heard Kate's final speech as a 'masterpiece

[93]

of dramatic irony'[22], indicating a heroic and undiminished resistance in defeat. While the emphases on torture and brutality were derived partly from the contemporary atrocities of the British in Northern Ireland, and reflected the awesome power of state violence, Marowitz also had in mind histories of endurance and unbroken resistance from, for example, the Stalinist period in the Soviet Union. Standing in chains below Petruchio's huge tribunal chair, Kate appeared, against all the odds, 'wasted and white but unbeaten'.[23]

Marowitz's *Shrew*, like his other collage versions of Shakespeare, was intended not as a revision or reinterpretation of the play, but rather as 'a head-on confrontation with the intellectual substructure of the play, an attempt to test or challenge, revoke or destroy the intellectual foundation which makes a classic the formidable thing it has become'. Such experiments can 'combat the assumptions of a classic with a series of new assumptions and force it to bend under the power of a new polemic' (*Marowitz Shakespeare*, p. 24). The reconstruction inevitably invites comparison with the original play, and in this respect it is clear that Marowitz's adaptation attenuates the variety and complexity, the multiplicity of perspectives encoded in the original textual inscriptions; it deprives the play of all humour, subtlety and pluralistic potentiality for interpretation. What remains or is recreated, seems very much a passive vehicle of directorial domination, as testified by the multiplicity of details linking the collage to the cultural ambience and *causes célèbres* of the 1960s – torture, brainwashing, madness, trials, institutionalisation. What Marowitz succeeded in doing was to arrest the smooth process of reinterpretation and appropriation which makes a classic text appear independent of the culture in which it is being remade, and to demand, in the spirit of a radical inventiveness possible only in the conditions of alternative and fringe theatre, that the assumptions underlying cultural monuments like Shakespeare plays need from time to time to be subjected to radical interrogation.

CHAPTER V

Jonathan Miller (1980)

I

The BBC/Time-Life Shakespeare series, which between 1979 and 1986 broadcast the entire canon of thirty-seven Shakespeare plays, was in its ambitious scope, scale and massive investment of cultural capital the most significant intervention to date into the reproduction of Shakespeare in performance. The series could not have been mounted at all without other more material investment: the BBC entered into partnership with the American company Time-Life TV, which in turn raised financial backing for the series from three big private corporations in the USA – the Exxon Corporation, Metropolitan Life Assurance and the Morgan Guaranty Trust Company of New York. This alliance between the British national communications medium and American private enterprise sufficiently indicates the economic and political origins of the project. It would naturally be foolish to write the series off as a predictable symptom of its capitalistic origins: but it is important to trace and measure the constraints and determinants built into the series itself as a consequence of its cultural and institutional basis.

The scale of investment and the nature of commercial underwriting (as distinct from commercial *sponsorship*) imposed one very obvious requirement on this enterprise: it should be economically

[95]

viable – that is, give a direct financial return, as well as a cultural pay-off, on commercial investment. This condition necessarily entailed the preservation of the plays in consumer-durable (video-cassette) form rather than reduction to one-off transmission, and an international marketing operation. Conscious of this dependence on the market rather than on patronage and subsidy, the planners insisted that productions should aim for 'high quality' and 'durability'. What 'high quality' originally implied in such a context is predictable: 'great' directors, 'classical' actors, 'straightforward' productions – 'these productions will offer a wonderful opportunity', said the first Executive Producer Cedric Messina, 'to study the plays performed by some of the greatest classical actors of our time.'[1] The notion of 'high quality' entailed in practice a conservative respect for 'traditional' values in Shakespearean production. Jonathan Miller, who is known for his theatrical work as an innovative and experimental director, described some of the 'problems' he inherited in taking over the series, among them 'the original contract with the American co-producers – it had to be so-called traditional . . .'[2] Cedric Messina had accepted this constraint with enthusiasm, in the belief that only 'traditional' productions would 'stand the test of time': 'We've not done anything too sensational in the shooting of it – there's no arty-crafty shooting at all. Some of them are, for want of a better word, straightforward productions.'[3] Despite his expressed reservations Jonathan Miller accepted the Executive Producership of the series after the second season (i.e. 1980-81): and directed productions of *Othello, Antony and Cleopatra, Troilus and Cressida, Timon of Athens* and *The Taming of the Shrew*.

II

As we have seen, Zeffirelli's film version dropped the 'Induction' in favour of an elaborate deployment of filmic devices providing an alternative establishing context. The BBC/Time-Life production also dispensed completely with Christopher Sly, though it opens with a gestural scenario of realistic establishing details: a stage-set city street with bits of Renaissance local colour such as dwarfs and jugglers. The absence of the 'Induction' from the BBC version provoked in this case more reaction from critics and reviewers, particularly since the entire series is understood to represent a partially-enforced commitment to certain 'classic' virtues, such as the retention of 'complete' or at least 'full' texts. The cut provoked Stanley Wells to some asperity:

> Jonathan Miller – acting, we must hope, in defiance of his literary consultant John Wilders – offered a simplified version of *The Taming of the Shrew* in this BBC production. To omit the Christopher Sly episodes is to suppress one of Shakespeare's most volatile lesser characters, to jettison most of the play's best poetry, and to strip it of an entire dramatic dimension. In a series announcing itself as 'The Complete Dramatic Works of William Shakespeare' this leaves a serious gap.[4]

In the BBC text of the play issued to accompany the series, the literary consultant actually discusses the absent 'Induction', observing only that it was 'omitted from this production as being unsuitable for the medium of television'.[5] The director held this view:

> I find the Christopher Sly 'Induction' terribly hard to do in any other format but the stage: it is a stage device, and it's frightfully hard to see it on television. It's a device that brings the audience into close identification with some person who is like them. It would be on television a little extra programme tagged on before the programme proper begins. On the stage it's possible to make it work much better: it's a folk style which sits rather uncomfortably in this very twentieth-century medium of domestic viewing.[6]

There seems to have been within the corporative consensus little disagreement with this line. Henry Fenwick, who assembled production notes on each play in the series, evidently approved: 'The only cut Miller took was to remove the "Induction" – that odd and unresolved framework of the beggar Sly being duped and entertained by a wealthy lord. Its removal is by no means new, and not only did it tidy the play considerably, it also helped the seriousness of the approach' (BBC *Shrew*, p. 18). Further endorsement of Miller's preference can be found in some interesting comments from the man directly responsible for the text, script editor David Snodin:

> In the television production of *The Taming of the Shrew* Jonathan Miller and I decided after considerable discussion to omit the whole of that curious, lengthy and disappointingly unresolved opening known as the 'Induction'. We made this decision for the following reasons: firstly, because we felt that it may confuse the viewer

coming to the play for the first time, very possibly to the detriment of his enjoyment of the play as a whole; secondly, because it is an essentially theatrical device which, while it has been known to work well in a theatre before a live audience, would not come across successfully in the very different medium of television; and lastly, because it is a device which presents the play's characters as 'actors', and we felt that this would hinder the attempt, in this production, to present them as real people in a real, and ultimately quite serious situation. (BBC *Shrew*, p. 30)

The range of motives underlying this contentious decision include some attenuated legacy (if Henry Fenwick's concept of 'tidiness' has any intellectual content at all) of neo-classical theory; a conviction that television and theatrical conventions are radically dissimilar and should be kept firmly separated; a paternalistic concern for the intelligibility threshold of the uneducated viewer; a curious notion that realism of presentation is a precondition of 'seriousness' in thematic approach; and an unwillingness to expose by any alienating or metadramatic devices the theatrical mechanisms of the play's construction.

Some of these shaping influences indicate contradictory pressures inherited from the institutional context of the series itself: from the constraints imposed by the American sponsors and co-producers, and from the economic and cultural imperatives of aiming at a world-wide market. It is quite clear that in this particular case the demand for accessibility and the censorship of innovation and experiment, both imposed by the American backers, led to an infringement of that other institutional stipulation, that the series should offer authentic and authoritative versions of the plays. The director's own position *vis-à-vis* those inherited conditions was also a somewhat contradictory one: known for his theatrical work as a particularly innovative, risk-taking cultural entrepreneur, he agreed to preside as Executive Producer over a series more remarkable for its relentlessly monumental classicising than for its creativity in the production of Shakespeare. His observations quoted above about the *Shrew* also appear contradictory: anxious to dissuade the viewer from identifying with Christopher Sly, he nonetheless apparently wanted to secure a seamless realism of presentation for a serious drama of domestic issues.

Whatever his capacities as a stage director, Miller believes in the absolute determinacy of the television medium, which he sees as imposing its own constraints on dramatic production. Television is incurably naturalistic and translates everything it touches into naturalism: 'as soon as you put Shakespeare on that box where ... people are accustomed to seeing naturalistic events represented, you are more or less obliged to present the thing as naturally as you can'.[7] Miller is therefore averse to any attempt to theatricalise television: TV productions should display no manneristic theatrical styles, no expressionistic acting and no mixing of conventions. This distinction between theatre and television as media of production is held to be absolute :

> There is something about television that makes it not altogether friendly to the enterprise of the Shakespearean drama ... there is something about the character and intrinsic structure of the plays, whether intended or not, which means that they sit rather uncomfortably on anything but the unfurnished set which seems appropriate to such writing. Television forces you into a more pictorial and scenic manner than I think is good for Shakespeare. (Miller in *The Shakespeare Myth*, 1988, p. 196)

Miller believes that there is no possibility of transferring theatrical structure and energy from the open space of the play's originating context to the closed interiority of the television screen:

> The point of an Elizabethan theatrical space – or indeed of any theatrical space – is that it is inseparable from the audience space with which it articulates. The whole point about the space of the unfurnished theatre-in-the-round is that the panoramic 360° circumference of the stage includes the circumference of the audience; both sit inside the same space. This relationship is instantly lost as soon as you are no longer sharing the space with the spectacle you are watching. The television is not inside a space at all: it's a notional space inside a box.
>
> When you sit inside the same space as the performance, there's a clearly intelligible margin to the area of the action which distinguishes it from the audience space. The edge of the television screen is not comparable to that, because the edge of the screen doesn't define a boundary that separates you the audience from it the spectacle; it merely marks off the set from the rest of your room.
>
> As soon as you present Shakespeare on television with real people it insists upon scenery, simply because the abstract space, which is said to be as possible on television as anywhere else, is quite different from the abstract space of the theatre: because it exists in a beyond to which you don't have any access at all. You can argue that the audience have no access to the stage either, because they are embarrassed or prevented by decorum from walking onto the stage. That is a matter of convention: in television you cannot walk into that space, and it doesn't change its appearance as you change the position of your head. You are not looking at a world happening: you are looking at a picture. (Miller in *The Shakespeare Myth*, 1988, pp. 196-7)

Together, then, the undeniable institutional constraints of the BBC series, and what were seen by the producers as the formal constraints of the television medium, produce an adherence to pictorial naturalism of presentation which is admitted as a commitment to illusionist representation. Hence the imperative necessity of ditching the self-reflexive and metadramatic potentialities of the Christopher Sly framework, which exists precisely to disrupt the stability of viewpoint upon which the imaginative totality of naturalism depends. There is no reason whatsoever why the 'Induction' and Sly-frame should not be adapted for television: but the result would be a different kind of television from that standardised as a norm in the BBC series. In Miller's view, the television audience should be protected fom any such complexity of awareness: they should be 'unaware of the fact that they're in the presence of an art-form' (Miller in Hallinan, p. 134).

III

These naturalistic premises find their detailed counterpart in the broadly naturalistic techniques of the production itself: though as we shall see, there are some interesting exceptions to this general definition. As I have already mentioned in relation to the opening scene, the play is set according to principles of naturalistic design, with one set simulating a populous Padua street, and others representing various domestic interiors. The basic principles of costume design were of course prescribed by the contract with the American co-producers – 'traditional'; that is, contemporary with Shakespeare's own time or with the historical period in which the play's action is set. In the case of the *Shrew*, this amounts more or less to the same thing; so the costumes are historically-accurate early-to mid-seventeenth-century bourgeois dress, incorporating some deliberate allusions to Renaissance visual sources.

In so far as set and costume design employed naturalistic conventions, the photographic techniques used complemented that stylistic medium. Long shots were used to represent the open street scenes, medium shots for small groupings of characters, and close-ups for moments of detailed psychological description. The typical shot, used recurrently throughout the production, is the close-up of one or more characters, using a telephoto lens, so that other characters, or gestural details of social activity, can be glimpsed out of focus behind or between the talking heads. The camera-position expresses precisely the relationship between the individual and society characteristic of bourgeois–liberal ideology: with the person fully-focused, concrete and massive; and the social environment gesturally present as 'background', but distanced and blurred. One particularly effective use of this technique involved the grouping of several characters – typically, a number of scheming, calculating men – around the camera, confiding and negotiating, with the outside world suspiciously excluded. Miller reinforced this effect by introducing a diminutive extra who would curiously penetrate the tightly-bunched circle of men to eavesdrop and pry (see illustration of I.i. *BBC 'Shrew'*, p. 42).

Almost consistently, the production employs the fourth-wall convention of a naturalistic stage-set, with the characters wholly absorbed in and confined to their reconstructed historical reality. Very occasionally this illusion is disrupted, by a character addressing the camera direct and thus fracturing the transparent fourth wall of the camera's perspective. The only characters permitted to do this are those on the fringes of the main action – characters such as Tranio and Hortensio – who can thus be considered as 'low-life' or comic characters, able to move off the elevated plane of theatrical realism and occupy the downstage area of more direct communication with the audience. Furthermore they are only allowed the opportunity of direct address when the text leaves them alone on stage with the responsibility of uttering an 'aside', that could be delivered to no conceivable object but the audience-camera (e.g. Tranio at II.i.396-403; this and all subsequent references in this chapter to the BBC text). Where on the other hand Petruchio is left alone on stage and given lines in soliloquy – such as his manifestos of strategy at II.i.167 : 'Say that she rail; why then I'll tell her plain . . .' and IV.i.172: 'Thus have I politicly begun my reign . . .', John Cleese delivered the speeches not as asides or direct addresses to the audience, but as meditative self-communings, introverted self-interrogations absorbedly unaware of listeners or spectators. The result is to transform speeches which must in the Elizabethan theatres have been offered direct to the audience for debate and consideration, into naturalistic representations of a psychological process of self-examination and moral inquiry.

The waspish review by Stanley Wells, already quoted, rebukes the prosaic, literalistic mode of presentation': though not, apparently, for its realism but for its artificiality – 'We opened on a stagey Italianate marketplace ...' (Wells, *Times Literary Supplement*, 1980). On the other hand Wells reserves high praise for another aspect of Miller's production style, his propensity to evolve a visual design in imitation of well-known classic paintings, in this case the domestic interiors of Dutch genre-painting: 'Baptista's house had lovely interiors reminiscent of Vermeer....' This observation and its tone were echoed in several other reviews: Sean Day-Lewis in the *Daily Telegraph* praised the 'beautifully-lit Vermeer interiors', and Chris Dunkley in the *Financial Times* thought the 'Dutch school interiors ... were beautiful'.[8] This technique is not only a particular personal enthusiasm of Jonathan Miller's: extensively used in other BBC productions (notably those directed by Elijah Moshinsky) it has come to be recognised almost as an aspect of 'house-style'. Elsewhere Stanley Wells guardedly concurs with some remarks made by John Wilders on the subject of this 'painterly' technique:

> The television screen resembles the stage in that it depicts characters who move and speak, but its two-dimensional surface, rectangular shape and surrounding frame also make it look like a picture. This is the feature of the small screen which has been exploited by Jonathan Miller, whose version of *Antony and Cleopatra* was designed to recall the paintings of Veronese, and by Elijah Moshinsky, whose *All's Well* contained visual quotations from Rembrandt and Vermeer. It is, I am sure, the most satisfactory answer the directors have yet found. It calls attention to the artifice of the plays and does justice to those tableaux which are as much a part of Shakespeare's dramatic language as his dialogue.[9]

If this method is, as Wilders suggests, a genuinely self-reflexive technique, laying bare the device of the production's visual design, then it must necessarily conflict, in the case of Miller's *Taming of the Shrew*, with the naturalistic principles of the director's conception. Interestingly, Miller's own views of its function are radically different from those of his colleague: for him the reconstruction of Renaissance visual sources is not a way of alienating the realism of the presentation, but a means of access to the historical reality the plays are conjectured to have been depicting. The Renaissance knew nothing, Miller believes, of our modern archaeological conception of a historical past, such as Rome or Egypt: they constructed their own images of other times and places, and those images are to be found recorded in contemporary paintings: 'Pictures of the period are the best documentary sources to go by in order to come up with something which convincingly recreates the world that Shakespeare or any other writer of the period is actually referring to' (Miller in Hallinan, p. 137). The most effective method of recreating that 'sixteenth-century imagination' is therefore to compose costume, *mise-en-scène* and action by analogy with sixteenth-century paintings.

Miller evidently encountered some difficulties in finding appropriate visual sources for a sixteenth-century English historical vision of a contemporary Italian setting:

> What I wanted was to get something which gave us a picture of domestic life at the start of the seventeenth century. Now, unfortunately, there are very few art historical sources which give us a view of life in the Italian interior. The Italians did not, in fact, go in for domestic genre paintings in the seventeenth century. (Miller in Hallinan, p. 138)

Undaunted by this unfortunate historical oversight on the part of the Italian Renaissance, Miller simply drew together his quest for appropriate visual sources with his conception of the play (discussed in greater detail below) as a particularly Protestant, even Puritan exploration of 'the setting up of a sober household and the necessity of marital obedience': and found the solution in Dutch genre-painting of a somewhat later period:

> The Dutch were endlessly painting scenes of domestic interiors. So I, as it were, plundered the Dutch painters and transformed them in order to create an Italian interior using Dutch sources, modifying them in order to give the appearance of what an Italian interior might have been like.
>
> In the paintings of such Dutch artists as Vermeer, you have people who celebrated, almost in a religious way, the sanctity of the sober domestic life, which is, in fact, what these plays are about . . . I felt the Dutch Puritan interior would be a good point from which to take off. (Miller in Hallinan, p. 138)

Which, then, is the more appropriate definition of Miller's painterly style – his own sense of visual imitation as a means of representing historical reality; or John Wilder's notion of visual quotation as a self-reflexive and metadramatic method of alienating realistic illusion? What precisely is the relationship between television naturalism and the patently conventional device of composing designs after the Great Masters? The solution to this apparent paradox lies in the peculiar history and status of naturalist conventions in the theatre. Classic theatrical naturalism is associated with the scrupulously-documented and pedantically-designed box-set interiors of Ibsen and Shaw, which come closest to realistic presentation: though even there the picture-frame stage, proscenium arch, orchestra pit and footlights unmistakably signify the conventional nature of these devices. An exterior location in a naturalistic production entails the use of patently artificial devices such as pictorial scenery, illuminated cyclorama, real or simulated vegetation on stage, choruses of real bullfrogs and corncrakes, and so on: techniques which differ strikingly from the apparently innocent conveying of reality by television, yet which have in theatrical contexts been acceptable as significations of reality. Miller's 'painterly' method of composition is actually an extension of these conventions: with the television screen's perimeter sealing off its brightly-lit image from the distracting emptiness of exterior space, in the manner of a proscenium arch; actors wearing costumes which can be regarded either as historically naturalistic, or conventionally *naturalised*, the familiar accoutrements of Shakespearean drama; and sets, whether studio or location, pictorialised in perspective and in proportion to the actors. Visual allusions to the Great Masters do not in any sense rupture the illusions of naturalism, but rather operate to confirm the illusory 'reality' of this familiar Shakespearean world; while simultaneously, for the cultivated elite capable of recognising such allusions, stamping on the productions a hallmark of high culture. This aspect of the production differs remarkably, as my previous observations (see above, pp, 61-4) have indicated, from Zeffirelli's deployment of similar techniques of visual presentation.

IV

Although Jonathan Miller always appears to have a strong and clearly-formulated intellectual conception of a production, his theoretical approach to acting is not what we normally associate with 'director's theatre'.

> I usually have a *general* idea, then let it shape up as I find the people. The people have a very strong material influence on what the play

is going to be. Whatever ideas you have about them are very often altered by the actual substance that is going to embody them, and there is no way you can impose an idea on an actor who is going to play it. Obviously one has to give them a general idea to which they must consent in order to work, but the moment to moment details of a production are very much determined by what they bring to it. And if you've got really good and talented actors they always bring an unprecedented thing . . .

It's always said by literary critics that you ought to be able to know what a character is from the sum of all that is actually said in a play by that given character; but if that were the case, then every time the play is performed the character would be the same. What is so peculiar about a play is that every time it's performed by a different actor, under the guidance of a different director, you're actually meeting someone quite new. As director, in order to find what is meant by a particular sentence, you and the actor have to improvise what that particular person means by the sentence they're using. And you can't do that until you've somehow invented a biography for them; in the end you have to invent a person not entirely made up of all the things they say in the play. (Miller quoted in BBC *Shrew*, pp. 20-1)

Clearly this is no simple theory of naturalism in acting: underlying these comments are quite sophisticated notions about language and communication, and a recognition that in performance 'character' is not something keyed into the words of a text and released by the actor's delivery, but rather a new entity over-determined by a complex process of exchange between text, director and actor, within the structural determinants of a concrete cultural situation. The actor is not a directorially-dominated *übermarionette*, but an independent seeker involved in a collaborative process of improvising character: '[Miller's] directing method . . . is to create an atmosphere where the actor is freed to release his own imagination instead of being obliged to play out a preconceived puppet role' (Day-Lewis, *Daily Telegraph*, 24 October 1980). Nonetheless, as the phrase about 'inventing a biography' suggests, what the actor's imagination is required to produce is a portrayal of character within a broadly naturalistic approach to representation. Even where the other elements of the dramatic narrative are patently non-naturalistic, the individual character's imaginary 'biography' can still be constructed.

It was from the outset fundamental to Miller's conception of the play that it is not a farce but a serious comedy. This entails, in his view, an understanding of the play as a direct address to serious moral problems of actual living, which could only be properly enacted through a medium of psychological realism. The farcical tradition in the play's performance was an inheritance to be escaped from, since it distorted the play's earnest contemplation of serious domestic issues:

> I think that *The Taming of the Shrew* has been bedevilled in the past by a lot of horseplay, a lot of rough-house and also a tremendously flamboyant, twinkle-eyed cavalier image of Petruchio, the gay, dashing cavalier that, 'By God, come kiss me, Kate', tames the young lass and brings her to heel. As with almost all of Shakespeare's comedies, it really is a more serious play than people have taken it for . . . as for Kate, I've always wanted to get away from this game, this twinkling, bridling, high-spirited young colt image of her. These things give the audience the impression that there's going to be a great deal more humour than, in fact, there is in the play. (Miller in Hallinan, pp. 138-9)

In Miller's view the play is a direct address to serious issues of sexual and family relationships, interpreted historically and approached moralistically:

> It's a play about many important themes in family life – fathers who distribute their love unfairly between their children and then are surprised to find that the deprived child is behaving cantankerously; the failure of men to recognise who the truly valuable woman is and who see in cantankerousness nothing but viciousness; the failure of unsophisticated lovers to see that the young and the bland is more likely to be the shrew than Kate herself. (Miller in Slater, p. 9)

These domestic themes are certainly conceived historically (see below), but the 'importance' attached to them by the director appears to owe something to an apparent transhistorical continuity of human experience: the 'themes' defined here are clearly not confined to a sixteenth-century social milieu. It is a natural progression from such an emphasis on immanent domestic experience to the view that psychological observations and interpretattions of contemporary modern behaviour can be applied retrospectively to a dramatisation of Renaissance values. The problem of 'shrewishness' raised by the play can then be understood in the light of current psychological theory: Petruchio becomes, in the words of one reviewer, 'an eccentrically pragmatic social worker using the wayward client's own doubtful habits to calm her down' (Dunkley, *Financial Times*, 24 October 1980). In an interview with Ann Pasternak Slater Miller was reminded that in rehearsal he had compared Petruchio's treatment of Kate with techniques of therapy for problem children used at the Tavistock clinic: 'There are ways in which a skilful therapist will gently mock a child out of a tantrum by giving an amusing imitation of the tantrum immediately after it's happened. The child then has a mirror held up to it and is capable of seeing what it looks like to others' (Miller in Slater, p. 11). At that point in the production where Petruchio refuses to allow Kate to keep the cap made for her (4.3) John Cleese performs exactly such an act of supposedly therapeutic, though potentially severely hurtful, mimicry.

The implications of such a psychological approach for actors leads us directly back to naturalism. If the character of Katherina is seen as a kind of case-study interpreted in the light of modern psychiatry, then the task of the actor is to present as accurately and convincingly as possible a simulation of the particular psychological deviance or disturbance imputed to Shakespeare's play. This is precisely what Sarah Badel, who plays Katherina, offers in the production: she appears constantly at the mercy of violent throes of infantile emotion, often completely possessed by passions of jealousy and resentment, and even in moments of greater stability appears close to the edge of neurotic excitation and hysteria. In the closing scene, completely cured by Petruchio's treatment, she displays an achieved serenity, a complete self-possession of confidence and poise. The 'imaginary biography' constructed for Katherina by Sarah Badel falls closely into line with the director's conception of the character:

> She's a woman of such passion, or that's how I saw it, a woman of such enormous capacity for love, that the only way she could be happy is to find a man of equal capacity. Therefore she's mad for lack of love . . . he feigns madness; she in my view is teetering on the edge of it. Petruchio is the only man who shows her what she's like. (quoted in BBC *Shrew*, p. 24)

The correct way to act this personality, it is inferred, is by means of an uninhibited self-abandonment to the inner truth of the role: 'There's no point in thinking about it or defending yourself with intelligent approaches – you simply have to come on with a total declaration and not care what anybody thinks at all, because she doesn't' (pp. 29-30). John Cleese is also quoted as complying with this general line of interpretation: he describes having consulted a psychiatrist who confirmed that the technique of mimicry and impersonation is in fact a perfect therapeutic treatment for 'shrews' (quoted in BBC *Shrew*, p. 23).

It is of course entirely possible that these illustrations of agreement between director and actors testify to a genuinely successful programme of collaboration: but it seems far more likely, given Miller's own intellectual and academic powers, that this unity of opinion was secured by an involuntary and painless process of directorial domination. And what Miller's presuppositions required happened to be what the actors were all too willing to provide: convincing naturalistic depictions of credible human behaviour. The achievement of realism was in turn abundantly rewarded by reviewers, always looking to be 'moved' and 'convinced' by accurate representations of 'life'. Stanley Wells: 'John Cleese's . . . was a deeply thoughtful performance, convincing us of the seriousness of Petruchio's intentions. . . . their relationship became a wholly credible process of mutual adjustment' (Wells, *Times Literary Supplement*, 31 October 1980). Or Chris Dunkley: 'Miller succeeded: the story did seem less deeply misogynistic than usual, more like a single peculiar case history and less of a general attack on women' (Dunkley, *Financial Times*, 24 October 1980).

What then happens to Miller's naturalistic propensities when they are applied to the self-evidently ostentatious artifice of the Bianca-plot? What scope is there for realism of characterisation in the context of a highly formalised Italianate comic structure? The contradiction posed here was certainly grasped very firmly in the director's mind:

> The plot of Bianca and her suitors is . . . a conventional piece of sixteenth-century artificial comedy. It's not realistic. And the great mastery of Shakespeare is his ability to show what seemed to be perfectly realistic human temperaments at work, inside the framework of a brightly-coloured, simplified jack-in-the-box, old-fashioned plot. You have to come head-on into that plot and be as straightforward and intense as you possibly can. Make each character go hell-for-leather for his or her own intention; play it with deadly seriousness, and farce will emerge from that. (Miller in Hallinan, p. 139).

Such a method will of course produce different results in different cases, and some of the results are unlikely to be naturalistic: as in the instances for example of purely comic characters whose 'imaginary biographies' could never be anything other than single-dimensional caricatures. But even in this context a certain measure of realism was encouraged. Susan Penhaligon, who plays Bianca, shows how under Miller's tutelage it was possible to construct a biography even for the part of Bianca:

> With Jonathan everybody is important. I know every director will *say* that but when it comes down to rehearsing, because of time or whatever, a lot of directors don't put it into practice. Jonathan does. He creates an atmosphere where you can go up to him at any time and talk for half an hour about your character – even if you've got two lines he'll build up a whole background for you so you know what you're saying. (quoted in BBC *Shrew*, p. 21)

In this particular case that 'background' proves to be a 'how many children had Lady Macbeth' biography of Bianca: 'she is as strong as Kate but had probably dealt with the family situation better than Kate: she'd learned to get her own way by smiling . . . Bianca was spoiled', and so forth. This example illustrates what seems to have been an instinctive consensus between director and actors in this production: an easy reconciliation of a particular directorial conception with the naturalistic presumptions and propensities of actors themselves. The interpretative result was recognised as identical with Miller's explicit intentions; Bianca was greeted by critics as a spoiled child who masks her spite and self-interest with a facade of sweetness. The corollary of Miller's sympathetic revaluation of the role of Katherina is that another woman should be obliged to bear the title of 'shrew'.

It is hardly surprising that other figures of the sub-plot proved rather less adaptable to the dominant naturalistic style. Miller's casting appears to have been an explicit acknowledgement of this, since he fitted a team of very well-known comic actors – familiar especially from numerous and frequent television appearances – with the roles of Gremio, Tranio, Hortensio, and the Pedant. These characters were all recognised by reviewers as playing appropriately within the discourses of comedy and farce: 'some of the performers', Stanley Wells noted, 'elected for a stylised, consciously comic mode' (Wells, *Times Literary Supplement*, 31 October 1980). Other critics drew the inevitable parallels with the familiar television forms of humorous sketch and situation-comedy: 'There was something of Capt. Peacock in *Are You Being Served?* about Frank Thornton's vain Gremio, a touch of Reginald Perrin's boss C.J. about John Barron's commanding Vincentio, and the fruits of many familiar comedy sketches in John Bird's fuss-pot Pedant' (Day-Lewis, *Daily Telegraph*, 24 October, 1980). It was clearly the director's intention, in casting so many inhabitants of television comedy, to mix the serious and comic modes within the production. In doing so he permitted the Bianca-plot to approach perilously close to exactly the kind of self-reflexiveness the production team was so determined to avoid:

> Actors in lesser roles descended to the kind of half-hearted improvisation which may be useful in rehearsal but should be expunged in performance: *'cum privilegio ad imprimendum solum*, i'n it, eh?' said Biondello; and the Pedant added 'was that all right?' to one of his comic inventions. (Wells, *Times Literary Supplement*, 31 October 1980)

As we have seen in an earlier quoted passage (above, p. 20) the production earned the condemnation of the same critic for permitting dramatic modes to be mixed at all. Those aspects of Miller's directing that approach more nearly to the spirit of Elizabethan stage practice again meet the reproof of an attenuated and irrelevant neo-classical criticism.

The most inspired, and in my view the most successful reconciliation of these serious and farcical tendencies, was the casting of John Cleese as Petruchio. Cleese was of course the best-known comic performer in the cast, a veteran of such brilliantly innovative television comedy programmes as *Monty Python's Flying Circus* and *Fawlty Towers*. Miller's motive for casting Cleese in a production dedicated to rediscovering seriousness in the *Shrew* seems to have been a gamble that paid off. Stanley Wells, as we have seen, found the portrayal 'deeply thoughtful . . . convincing us of the seriousness of Petruchio's intentions' (Wells, *Times Literary Supplement*, 31 October 1980); while Sean Day-Lewis found the 'fortuitous reference back to the distracted existence of Basil Fawlty and his shrewish wife' – ('be she as old as Sybil . . .') – to be 'no disadvantage'. One reviewer suggested that the collision of serious and comic modes in Cleese's performance may not have been fortuitous at all:

> Its success was due not to a decision to treat Petruchio comically, but to Miller's perception that the Basil Fawlty persona which is John Cleese's distinctive role has a terrible kind of manic seriousness. This Cleese brought with him, with the result that a steely, authentically puritanical – almost Cromwellian – character emerged.[10]

Notwithstanding these various attempts to reconcile the serious and the comic within a unified style, the distinction of the performance seems to me to reside in the distancing and doubleness of Cleese's delivery. His performance stands out from those characterisations which hew closely to naturalism, as a sustained and inspired deployment of Brechtian alienation-effect. Cleese is never entirely naturalised within his role, as other comic characters contrive to be: his delivery of the lines always preserves a certain ironic distance, as if he found difficulty not only in taking them seriously himself, but in the idea that anyone possibly could take them seriously at all. The result is a beautifully-composed detachment, which allows to the part of Petruchio a unique doubleness and self-reflexive ironical consciousness. Towering above his strange mixed company of Stanislavskian soul-searchers and music-hall comedians in creative innovation as well as in height, Cleese is easily the most admirable component of the production.

V

Compared with Michael Bogdanov's RSC production, Miller's BBC version is in terms of ideology, historiography and sexual politics a much more 'establishment' production, overtly moralising and even religious, committed to decoding the 'taming' story as the fable of a companionate marriage disciplined by the ideal of the ordered family. As we have already seen, both directors have claimed that their respective productions were based on, and informed by, a serious effort to understand the play *historically*. But Jonathan Miller adopted a radically different historical perspective, and is openly contemptuous of the kind of historicism represented by Bogdanov's approach: he argues that it is 'irresponsible and silly' to make the *Shrew* into 'a feminist tract' (Miller interviewed in *The Shakespeare Myth*, 1988, p. 200).

Miller's production was based on his reading of a particular kind of historiography: he cites as specific sources Lawrence Stone's *The Family, Sex and Marriage, 1500-1800*, and Michael Walzer's *The Revolution of the Saints*, about the rise of Puritanism. Miller follows the French *annales* historians in a search for the *mentalité* of a particular society: a search which should remain unaffected by modern views on the content of such historically-constituted ideologies. We can understand a period like the Elizabethan only by acknowledging the difference and distance between their *men-*

talité and our own. In Miller's view the play is expressive of a peculiarly Renaissance vision of the harmonious marriage within the orderly society: 'its spirit derives from Elizabethan Puritanism's view of the household as an orderly place in which the marriage is consecrated not in the church but in the orderly procedures of domesticity; in which obedience is required, not in order to preen the male pride of the father, but to restore order in a fallen world' (Miller in *The Shakespeare Myth*, p. 201). In Miller's view, then, the problems posed by the 'taming' story are to be resolved not by reference to modern feminism, but to contemporary Renaissance thought on the nature of marriage, the family and the state. In the production this context was particularly emphasised by having the assembled company in the final scene sing together a psalm celebrating the virtues of family life, to secure a formal declaration of reconciliation and harmony.

Where Michael Bogdanov relied on a fairly traditional Marxist–existentialist understanding of history, Jonathan Miller drew on newer developments in historiography, on the work of social historians more prepared to grant a relative autonomy to cultural practice, and to acknowledge the material reality of ideology. In sharing the social historian's concern with cultural life, with the affective structures of kinship, family and marriage, Miller occupies a historiographical ground which meshes more effectively with the dramatic worlds of Shakespeare's plays than the simplifications of vulgar-Marxism. Furthermore, in insisting, for any theatrical reconstruction of the *mentalité* of Tudor England, on a clarification of historical distance, Miller appears in sympathy with trends in historical criticism which have sought to undermine the concept of Shakespeare's plays as a repository of immutable values, to acknowledge the pastness of the past, and to secure a knowledge of history through difference. As we shall see, this apparent link with the 'New Historicism', though it lends a sophistication to Miller's arguments, is merely superficial; and in fact his intellectual heritage is rather the 'old historicism' of Tillyard, mediated through Cambridge scholarship and historiography. Although, as the titles suggest, there are continuities here, there are also crucial differences between the two schools. The traditional historicism sought, under a guise of academic neutrality, to detach from the past images of organic unity, such as Tillyard's 'Elizabethan world picture'; while the New Historicism exposes those images as polemical gestures, and seeks to recover the past as a site of contradiction and of economic and political struggle. The old historicism denied any political engagement or contemporary application; while the New Historicism openly acknowledges the political dispositions of all historical criticism, including its own. Miller belongs to the former rather than the latter position (see Miller in *The Shakespeare Myth*, 1988, p. 199).

Whether or not Miller's production may be considered genuinely historical can remain open to debate: but it is certainly not feminist. He has said frequently that he thinks the play has nothing to do with modern feminism: that a return to an imaginative world of the past requires the elimination of such contemporary preoccupations.

> Take *The Taming of the Shrew*. I think it's an irresponsible and silly thing to make that play into a feminist tract: to use it as a way of proving that women have been dishonoured and hammered flat by male chauvinism. There's another, more complex way of reading it than that: which sees it as being their particular view of how society ought to be organised in order to restore order in a fallen world. Now we don't happen to think that we are inheritors of the sin of Adam and that orderliness can only be preserved by deputing power to magistrates and sovereigns, fathers and husbands. But the fact that they did think like that is absolutely undeniable, so productions which really do try to deny that, and try to hi-jack the work to make it address current problems about womens' place in society, become boring, thin and tractarian. (Miller in *The Shakespeare Myth*, 1988, p. 200)

To read a sixteenth-century play in the light of contemporary feminist preoccupations is in Miller's view to deny its historical reality, its pastness; and to translate the foreign language of the past into a familiar modern idiom is to lose sight of its historical veracity.

> I had to give it an explicitly religious format, so people could see it not as just the high-jinks of an intolerantly selfish man who was simply destroying a woman to satisfy his own vanity, but a sacramental view of the nature of marriage, whereby this couple had come to love each other by reconciling themselves to the demands of a society which saw obedience as a religious requirement. (Miller in *The Shakespeare Myth*, 1980, p. 200)

The correct approach to such a play is thus a form of cultural archaeology, or to use Miller's own term 'ethnology': 'One of the reasons we do these plays is because they are a form of ethnology. How did they live? What did they actually value? What did they cherish? What obligations did they feel were binding?' (Miller in *The Shakespeare Myth*, 1988, p. 201). Both feminist sexual politics and Marxist historiography distort the historical reality of these institutions and relationships: a different kind of historical psychology is needed to appreciate the concrete human texture of the lived experience embodied in the play:

> I also feel that it is very simple-minded for a sort of crude *Time Out* marxism to say well, of course, the reason why they thought that is because marriage was a salient on the broad front of advancing capitalism. Certainly there are ways in which the notions of inheritance and the conveyance of property was an important part of this, but I think that comes out of the play: there the economic and cultural considerations are married closely together. What naive modern marxism leaves out of consideration is the world and the life of the imagination: how did people actually view families, daughters, children . . . A father fails to recognise which daughter is the shrew: which shrew is being tamed? Katherina, or the well-loved younger daughter – who actually is much more shrewish, wayward and wilful than her sister? A purely marxist interpretation would leave out of consideration these purely affectional relationships between fathers and daughters. I suppose that in most of my work I've been prompted as much by considerations of the family as a purely affective structure as I have by families as complex institutions for preserving the status quo with regard to the inheritance and transfer of property.
> (Miller in *The Shakespeare Myth*, 1988, pp. 202-2)

Such ideas adopt a more familiar formulation when expressed, without the allusions to ethnology and *annales* historiography, in John Wilders's introduction to the BBC text. The attitudes to marriage and sexual relationship offered by the play are historic, and should not be considered from a contemporary modern perspective. Kate is no proto-feminist, resisting the power of patriarchy, but a model example of a successfully subdued woman:

> . . . she must subordinate her will to his. This is a belief with which few twentieth century audiences would agree and, for this reason, *The Taming of the Shrew* may well appear a repellently chauvinistic play. But it was a belief held by the vast majority of Shakespeare's own audience, especially those of the bourgeois, merchant class in the portrayal of which he took such care. He includes in the play their assumptions as well as their way of life. How far he himself agreed with them we cannot know; as always, he remains true to his characters, which is not necessarily the same thing as being true to his own beliefs. It is more than likely that he agreed with them.
> (Wilders in BBC *Shrew*, pp. 14-15)

The argument, we perceive, is E. M. W. Tillyard's: that largely discredited orthodoxy of the 1940s, which insisted on confining the Renaissance drama firmly within the parameters prescribed by the most orthodox and conservative forces within Tudor ideology: here sustained and consolidated by the BBC Shakespeare series. Shakespeare shared the convictions and opinions of his time and his class: if we define those Elizabethan views, we define the ideology of Shakespeare's plays. Given the opportunity to enlarge on and elaborate the historiographical context of his views on gender politics, Miller could sound exactly the same Tillyardian note:

> Shakespeare is the great playwright of the family. He had a very clear understanding of the political theology of the family and of the relationship of the family to the state. Shakespeare was very interested in the notion of authority within the state – and I believe that he underwrote the idea that the state, whether it was the small state of the family or the larger state of the country, required and needed the unquestioned authority of some sort of sovereign to whom everyone could defer . . .
>
> In *The Taming of the Shrew* we have something very similar in that Shakespeare is extolling the virtues of the obedient wife – not the subordinate, cowed and simply docile, crushed wife – in accordance with the sixteenth-century belief that for the orderly running of society, some sort of sacrifice of personal freedom is necessary.

The closing scene of the play is transformed by Miller (partly by the addition of the psalm mentioned earlier) into a model of social unity and domestic harmony.

> We've taken one of the psalms which talks about the orderliness and grace and beauty of the family. It's one of the Psalms that would have been sung in a household after a meal in a Puritan household [*sic*], and it somehow reconciles all the conflicts of the previous two hours. All these characters have been working at odds with each other, trying to get their own ends. Now they are suddenly brought together in what the sixteenth century regarded as *communitas*, which is the bringing together, the unifying and harmonising of all individual desires so that they actually work together rather than against one another. This is expressed beautifully when they all jointly sing a part song, which in itself is an expression of bringing different voices together in one harmonious performance. (Miller in Hallinan, pp. 140-1)

John Wilders makes the same point, linking the production's formal closure with its gender politics and its supposedly ideology-free academic historicism:

> It was in order to underline the play's religious as well as social

[115]

defence of matrimony that Jonathan Miller . . . decided to conclude it with the singing of a Puritan hymn, a paraphrase of one of the psalms, in which marriage is celebrated not as a social convention but as a manifestation of the ideal relationship between man, woman and God. We shall misunderstand the play if we assume that Shakespeare is always, as he was called not long ago, 'our contemporary'. (BBC *Shrew*, p. 16)

That a play like *The Taming of the Shrew* could be designated as the invocation of such an 'ideal relationship' between man and woman will be a matter of some curiosity and no little surprise to many readers. Nonetheless it is evident that Miller's academic historicism has delivered a view of the play coincident with that tradition of 'liberal' domestication which has reconstructed the Shrew as a fable of companionate relationship. One measure of the production's success in endorsing that tradition is the substantial number of reviews which enthusiastically accepted Miller's view of the 'taming' process as a valid formula for nuptial mutuality. I have already quoted Chris Dunkley's view that the production made the play seem 'less misogynistic than usual'; and other similar tributes abound, from Stanley Wells's notion of the taming as 'a wholly credible process of mutual adjustment', to Sean Day-Lewis's echo of *Playboy* on Zeffirelli – 'she desires nothing more than a man so strong that she can decently grant him "love, fair looks and true obedience"' (Day-Lewis, *Daily Telegraph*, 24 October 1980).

Feminists would insist, quite correctly, that all this amounts rather to a compact of masculine understanding. I have argued that the play addresses issues of gender in such a way as to formulate an intervention into the sexual politics of its own time. I have also argued that the play in its received entirety does not propose any simple or unitary view of sexual politics: it contains a crudely reactionary dogma of masculine supremacy, but it also works on that ideology to force its expression into self-contradiction. The means by which this self-interrogation is accomplished is, however, that complex theatrical device of the Sly-framework, which is in Miller's production utterly abandoned. Without the metadramatic potentialities of the Sly-framework, any production of the *Shrew* is thrown much more passively at the mercy of the director's artistic and political ideology.

Miller consciously and explicitly denied the play any purchase on the sexual politics of the present, on the grounds that a focus on those would obscure apprehension of the historical experience.

But to deprive the *Shrew* of both its technical capacity for self-criticism (the Sly-frame) and its potentiality for contemporary application (as exploited by Bogdanov) is in practice to permit the sexual ideology which the play contains – a vision of marriage as the 'taming' of a woman by her prospective husband – a free and unhindered passage to the modern spectator. If the play can be shown to have spoken for the authority of men and the subordination of women, then genuinely historical analysis must acknowledge that: but if that historical analysis fails to engage with contemporary sexual politics, then the play will continue to speak, notwithstanding the best liberal intentions of its mediators, for the same repressive and authoritarian ideology.

Kate's closing speech of submission is delivered in this production as the expression of a new-found and hard-won serenity, the philosophy of a woman who is at peace with her husband and herself. The elaborate defence of hierarchy, of inequality, of masculine supremacy and feminine abjection, is offered to the assembled household in sober seriousness and with absolute conviction, and represents a clear expression of the director's moral and historical vision. The actress's understanding was rather different: for her the speech is primarily a language of private communication between Katherina and Petruchio. Henry Fenwick raised the matter with Sarah Badel:

> As for the final speech, the one that nowadays people find so hard to accept? 'You mean the speech to make Germaine Greer sick?', she says. 'That's a love speech to him. For the first time she realises the extreme vulnerability of men. She was so vulnerable herself before that she couldn't see it at all! . . .She's found release. That's how she finds her tongue at the end and can be eloquent.' (quoted in BBC *Shrew*, p. 25)

The long-standing tradition of liberal appropriation that regards this rhetorical speech of over forty lines as a simple private communication between husband and wife has never succeeded in convincingly explaining the immense distance between overt sense-meaning and imputed latent sub-text. Since the speech functions, even within this interpretation, as a demonstration of Petruchio's power, it is hard to see wherein his 'vulnerability' lies. And if when a woman finds the power of articulate speech she can express nothing more than a doctrine of masculine supremacy, it becomes difficult to accept this as the discovery of anything that could legitimately be called '*her* tongue'.

[117]

In the autumn of 1987 Jonathan Miller scored a hat-trick in his
association with *The Taming of the Shrew*, by directing it for the
Royal Shakespeare Company in Stratford's main-house
auditorium. It is perhaps all the more surprising, in the light of
this long association with the play, that this his most recent production contained so little that was new or surprising. The programme notes assembled a collage of documents, primary and secondary, endorsing orthodox Tudor views on marriage, the family,
the state, the subordination of women: so the production was
framed once again by the historiographical context of Miller's
BBC/Time-Life Shakespeare Series production.

The terms of that familiar, well-supported and cogently-argued
polemic are by now well-enough known. But it is not simply a
matter of modern feminist appropriation for *The Taming of the
Shrew* to be interpreted as a dialectic of patriarchal oppression and
feminine resistance. Miller's historicism is guilty of precisely the
same distortions and oversimplifications as that post-Tillyard
orthodoxy which took the most dogmatic and *ex cathedra* utter-
ances of church and state for a comprehensive formulation of
Tudor ideology. Yet it is evident from the very historians Miller
cites that there was within the period, as Catherine Belsey puts it,
'a contest for the meaning of the family ... which unfixed the
existing system of differences'. Such 'unfixing' of traditional
stereotypes brings temporarily into view the contradictions within
an institutional apparatus: and it is not at all unreasonable to see
The Taming of the Shrew as an exploration of this newly-visible
sexual ideology, accomplished in part by the dualities and ironical
perspectives of the Sly-framework. Miller however continues to
occlude these historical contradictions by imposing on the play a
unitary vision of Renaissance culture as a monolithic consensus
of shared orthodoxy.

The production methods employed to dramatise and embody
these historiographical ideas bear certain obvious similarities to
Miller's television production. The principal justification for aban-
doning the Christopher Sly framework from the BBC version was
that the 'Induction' is a stage device which cannot be made to

work on TV. Christopher Sly was also, however, banished from the Stratford version, and in his place Miller supplied interludes performed by a group of musicians costumed in a folksy version of the *commedia dell'arte*, playing snatches of old tunes in front of a white curtain. Mingling with the musicians appear a number of actors dressed in Elizabethan costume; there was an emphasis in the tableau on pleasant social intercourse between the sexes, the gaiety of a festival or holiday occasion. The performers were not, however, the travelling players of Shakespeare's 'Induction', but a mere device for inducting the spectator into a remarkably idealised version of Renaissance culture. The play is therefore stripped even of the possibilities for doubleness and alienation inscribed within the theatrical techniques of the Christopher Sly framework.

The production's set was another attempt, following the BBC version, to locate this understanding of the play into the visual perspective of a Renaissance city, mediated through a more abstract visual language. Certainly the set seemed constructed to express a director's and set-designer's vision, rather than to provide an adequate space in which actors might move. The stage was so steeply raked, and culminated in a ramp so acutely angled, as to render a simple entrance into a sliding scramble more akin to scree-running; and any upstage exit left had to begin with a preliminary dash, to gather the momentum necessary for a successful ascent. Most of the action was well downstage – probably as a simple consequence of the natural tendency of all objects, including actors and props, to roll downhill – but the effects of this 'fore-staging' were certainly significant. In a clear departure from the naturalistic idiom of the BBC version (in which only occasionally were a couple of characters like Tranio and Hortensio permitted the privilege of direct address-to-camera) most of the characters played out to the audience, with varying degrees of self-consciousness and arch, comic awareness. Played in this way, much of the action simply presented comedy directly for the audience's immediate approval, and elicited unfailingly the kind of mechanical laughter which Stratford main-house audiences are all too ready to provide: from the ripely-informed chuckles of those who laugh at jokes about 'cates' (which are about as funny as a footnote) to the hysterical aisle-rolling of those who, on hearing an idiom as simple and common as a Scots accent, cannot contain their urine.

The more subtle performance of Brian Cox as Petruchio involved a more complex (and considering the gender-political sensitivity of the play in question, more dangerous) relationship between actor and audience: one in which the audience is drawn, by a perilous combination of sexist freemasonry and engaging charm, into a direct complicity with the ultimate object of all the characters' strategies – to secure Katherina for Petruchio's wife. And an object Katherina remained, since she was the one character who was not privileged to address the audience, remaining confined (until her final speech of submission) within the inaccessible environment of her neurosis: an object of mockery, fear, desire, concern; a patient whose case, pronounced incurable, finds its way into the hands of a sympathetic and resolute psychotherapist.

It is possible that the term 'charm' used above of Brian Cox's performance has rarely been applied to an actor with the image of a craggy, macho Glaswegian heavy. Yet Cox is a 'charming' actor, both in terms of his ability to compel an audience's attention, and in the secondary sense of being able to offer to an audience's sympathy the irresistible presence of a humane, vulnerable, *likeable* individual. When Katherina had broken the lute over Hortensio's head, Cox held the shattered remnants in his hand and spoke of taming Katherina, while wincing with palpable apprehension. We were assured of the humanity of his motives, the seriousness of his intentions, the resolute courage of his determination to 'save' Katherina, to redeem her from the curse of her shrewish nature. The spectators were constituted not as witnesses to this process, but as sympathetic participants in a necessary mission of salvation. This style of performance appropriately occupies the theoretical nexus of Miller's interpretation: it is the point where his conception of Renaissance gender politics fuses with his modern psychologistic notions of character. But we are obliged to ask, in sober seriousness, what meanings are in practice delivered by such a combination of historiographical and contemporary preoccupations? I have already argued that this unitary view of Renaissance ideology is a radical oversimplification of what, historically, was a contest for meaning enacted between dominant and subordinate social groups. In terms of contemporary ideology, and in particular of the gender politics from which, for most of us, *The Taming of the Shrew* has become inseparable, the meanings of this production are simply unacceptable. Academic historicism cannot be regarded as a convenient means of evading urgent contemporary issues.

[120]

NOTES

Chapter I

1 The Folio text is the basis of all modern editions of *The Taming of the Shrew*. *The Taming of a Shrew* can be found in an old-spelling edition in Geoffrey Bullough, *Narrative and Dramatic Sources of Shakespeare*, Routledge and Kegan Paul, 1957, vol. 1; and in facsimile reproduction in Charles Praetorius's edition for the Shakespeare Society in 1886, from which my quotations and references are drawn. A 'memorial reconstruction' is a play-text put together by spectators and/or actors recalling a script from its stage performance.

2 See Thomas Kyd, *The Spanish Tragedy*, ed. Philip Edwards, Manchester University Press, 1977; Robert Greene (with Thomas Lodge), *A Looking-Glass for London and England*, ed. G. A. Clugston, Garland Publishing, 1980; and Robert Greene, *The Scottish History of James IV*, ed. Norman Sanders, Methuen, 1970.

3 The information used here derives from prompt-books in the records of the Shakespeare Memorial Theatre and Royal Shakespeare Company, held in the Shakespeare Centre Library, Stratford-upon-Avon. Martin Harvey's production is discussed in Tori Haring-Smith's invaluable stage-history, *From Farce to Metadrama: a stage history of 'The Taming of the Shrew', 1594-1983*, Greenwood Press, 1985, pp. 98-103, which also gives a full account of eighteenth-century adaptations.

4 Stratford productions in this category include: Robert Atkins (1946); Michael Benthall (1948); George Devine (1953); John Barton (1960); Trevor Nunn (1967); Barry Kyle (1982).

5 See Brian Morris (ed.), The New Arden Shakespeare: *The Taming of the Shrew*, London: Methuen, 1982, pp. 8-9.

6 See Ann Thompson, ed., The New Cambridge Shakespeare: *The Taming of the Shrew*, Cambridge University Press 1984.

7 Richard Hosley (ed.), The Pelican Shakespeare: *The Taming of the Shrew*, Harmondsworth: Penguin, 1964, revised 1970, p. 11.

8 Philip Edwards (ed.), The New Cambridge Shakespeare: *Hamlet*, Cambridge University Press, 1985 p 32.

9 For further discussion of *Henry V* in this context see Graham Holderness, Nick Potter and John Turner, *Shakespeare: The Play of History*, London: Macmillan, 1988, pp. 72-5.

10 Baptista's use of the word at I.i.97 contains, unintentionally on his part, both meanings of 'cunning'.

11 See Holderness, Potter and Turner, *The Play of History, passim*.

12 For an honourable exception see Robert Weimann, 'Mimesis in Ham-

let', in Patricia Parker and Geoffrey Hartmann (eds.), *Shakespeare and the Question of Theory*', London: Methuen, 1986.

13 For further discussion see Graham Holderness, *Hamlet*, Milton Keynes: Open University Press, 1987.

14 See John Barton, *Playing Shakespeare*, Methuen, 1986.

15 Stanley Wells,'A prosaic transformation', *Times Literary Supplement*, 31 October 1980.

16 A comprehensive review of recent feminist critical discussion of Shakespeare is to be found in Ann Thompson, '"The warrant of womanhood": Shakespeare and feminist criticism', in Graham Holderness (ed.), *The Shakespeare Myth*, Manchester University Press, 1988.

17 Christopher Hill, *The World Turned Upside Down*, 1972, Harmondsworth: Penguin, 1975, pp. 306ff.

18 See Lawrence Stone, *The Family, Sex and Marriage, 1500-1800*, 1977, abridged edition, Harmondsworth: Pelican, 1979.

19 Catherine Belsey, 'Disrupting sexual difference: meaning and gender in the comedies', in John Drakakis (ed.), *Alternative Shakespeares*, London: Methuen, 1986.

20 Juliet Dusinberre, *Shakespeare and the Nature of Women*, London: Macmillan. 1975, p. 104.

21 James Worsdale, *A Cure for a Scold*, 1735, facsimile, London: Cornmarket Press, 1969.

Chapter II

1 London *Evening Standard*, 22 June 1960.

2 Sally Beauman, *The Royal Shakespeare Company: a history of ten decades*, Oxford University Press, 1982, pp. 14-15.

3 Christopher J. McCullough, 'The Cambridge connection: towards a materialist theatre practice', in Graham Holderness (ed.), *The Shakespeare Myth*, Manchester University Press, 1988, p. 112. See also Alan Sinfield, 'Royal Shakespeare' in Jonathan Dollimore and Alan Sinfield (eds.) *Political Shakespeare*, Manchester University Press, 1985.

4 Terry Hands interviewed by Christopher J. McCullough in *The Shakespeare Myth*, 1988, p. 124.

5 David Addenbrooke, *The Royal Shakespeare Company*, William Kimber, 1974, p. 43.

6 Peter Hall, 'Shakespeare and the modern director', in *The Royal Shakespeare Company, 1960-1963*, Reinhardt, 1964, p. 44.

7 Peter Hall, 'A new way with Shakespeare', *Sunday Times*, 22 November 1959.

8 Peter Hall, 'Speech to the company', January 1963, *Royal Shakespeare Theatre Tapes*, Shakespeare Centre Library, Stratford-upon-Avon. Quoted in Addenbrooke (1974), p. 43.

9 See John Barton, interviewed in Addenbrooke (1974), p. 208. For the RSC and Cambridge English, see McCullough, *The Shakespeare Myth*, 1988.

10 Prompt-book for the Royal Shakespeare Company 1960 production

of *The Taming of the Shrew*, dir. John Barton, held in the Shakespeare Centre Library, Stratford-upon-Avon.

11 Bernard Levin, *Daily Express*, 22 June 1960.

12 Kenneth Tynan, *Observer*, 26 June 1960.

13 *Gloucestershire Echo*, 22 June 1960.

14 Gareth Lloyd Evans, *Stratford Herald*, 24 June 1960.

15 *Yorkshire Post*, 22 June 1960.

16 *Wolverhampton Express and Star*, 22 June 1960.

17 Robert Speaight, 'The 1960 season at Stratford-upon-Avon', *Shakespeare Quarterly*, XI, 1960, p. 447.

18 *Nottingham Guardian Journal*, 22 June 1960; *Manchester Guardian*, 23 June 1960.

19 See Graham Holderness, 'Boxing the bard: Shakespeare and television', in *The Shakespeare Myth*, 1988, pp. 183-4.

20 See Graham Holderness, 'The albatross and the swan: two productions at Stratford', *New Theatre Quarterly*, 14, 1988.

21 See McCullough on 'The Cambridge connection' in *The Shakespeare Myth*, 1988; and in the same volume, John Wilders and Jonathan Miller interviewed.

22 See Graham Holderness, 'Agincourt 1944: readings in the Shakespeare myth', in Peter Humm, Paul Stigant and Peter Widdowson (eds.), *Popular Fictions*, Methuen, 1987.

23 *Oxford Mail*, 22 June 1960.

24 *Daily Herald* and *Daily Sketch*, 22 June 1960.

25 Thomas Wiseman's 'Limelight', *Evening Standard*, 24 June 1960.

26 *Daily Mail*, 22 June 1960.

27 *The Times*, 22 June 1960.

28 T. C. Worsley, *Financial Times*, 22 June 1960.

29 Alan Dent, *News Chronicle*, 22 June 1960.

30 *Warwickshire Advertiser*, 25 June 1960.

31 *Daily Telegraph*, 22 June 1960.

32 Royal Shakespeare Company touring production of *The Taming of the Shrew*, 1985, dir. Di Trevis. Records in Shakespeare Centre Library, Stratford-upon-Avon.

33 Geraldine Cousin, 'The touring of the Shrew', *New Theatre Quarterly*, 2: 7, Cambridge University Press, August 1986, p. 280.

Chapter III

1 Catherine Belsey, 'Shakespeare and film', *Literature/Film Quarterly*, XI, Spring 1983, no.2.

2 Graham Holderness, 'Radical potentiality and institutional closure', in Jonathan Dollimore and Alan Sinfield (eds.), *Political Shakespeare*, Manchester University Press, 1985.

3 Andre Bazin, 'Theatre and cinema', in *What is Cinema?* 1967, vol. 1, p. 106.

4 Carey Harrison, *Sight and Sound*, 36, Spring 1967, p. 98.

5 Zeffirelli in a programme note for the Old Vic *Romeo and Juliet*, 1960;

quoted in Jill L. Levenson, *Shakespeare in Performance: Romeo and Juliet*, Manchester University Press, 1987, p. 85.

6 John Francis Lane, *Films and Filming*, October 1966, p. 50.
7 Richard Roud in the *Guardian*, 3 March 1967.
8 Jack J. Jorgens, *Shakespeare on Film*, Bloomington: Indiana University Press, 1979, p. 71.
9 See especially Mikhail Bakhtin, *Rabelais and his World*, trans. Helen Iswolsky, Cambridge, Mass.: CIT Press, 1968.
10 Quoted in A. P. Rossiter, *English Drama from Early Times to the Elizabethans*, New York: Barnes and Noble, 1967, pp. 64-5.
11 For further discussion of 'carnival' see C. L. Barber, *Shakespeare's Festive Comedy*, Princeton: Princeton University Press, 1959; Michael D. Bristol, *Carnival and Theatre*, Methuen, 1985: and Graham Holderness, *Shakespeare's History*, Dublin: Gill and Macmillan, 1985, pp. 79-87.
12 Roger Manvell, *Shakespeare and the Film*, South Brunswick and New York,: A. S. Barnes, 1971, 1979, describes the various locations used: p. 100.
13 Penelope Gilliatt, *Observer*, 5 March 1967.
14 Patrick Gibbs, *Daily Telegraph*, 28 February 1967.
15 Stephen Farber, *Film Quarterly*, XX, Fall 1967, no. 1, p. 61.
16 Tori Haring-Smith, *From Farce to Metadrama: a stage history of 'The Taming of the Shrew', 1594-1983*, Westport, Conn. and London: Greenwood Press, 1985.
17 Alexander Walker, *Evening Standard*, 2 March 1967.
18 David Robinson, *Financial Times*, 3 March 1967.
19 Penelope Houston, *Spectator*, 10 March 1967.
20 Felix Barker, *Evening News*, 2 March 1967.
21 *Monthly Film Bulletin*, XXXIV, April 1967, no. 399, p. 58.
22 *Evening Standard*, 5 July 1965.
23 *The Sun*, 28 February 1967.
24 *Playboy*, June 1967.
25 Robert Robinson, *Sunday Telegraph*, 5 March 1967.
26 Dilys Powell, *Sunday Times*, 5 March 1967.
27 Ian Christie, *Daily Mail*, 28 February 1967.
28 Gerald Kaufman, *Listener*, 9 March, 1967.
29 *Morning Star*, 4 March 1967.
30 *New Statesman*, 3 March 1967.

Chapter IV

1 See John Elsom and Nicholas Tomalin, *The History of the National Theatre*, Jonathan Cape, 1978, pp. 6-7.
2 See Sally Beauman, *The Royal Shakespeare Company: a history of ten decades*, Oxford University Press, 1982, pp. 8-11.
3 See David Addenbrook, *The Royal Shakespeare Company*, William Kimber, 1974, pp. 66, 182.
4 Alan Sinfield, 'Royal Shakespeare', in Jonathan Dollimore and Alan Sinfield (eds.), *Political Shakespeare*, Manchester University Press, 1985.

5 Trevor Nunn in Ralph Berry, *On Directing Shakespeare*, Croom Helm, 1977, p. 56.
6 Jan Kott, *Shakespeare our Contemporary*, 2nd edition, Methuen, 1967.
7 Jonathan Dollimore and Alan Sinfield, 'History and Ideology: the instance of Henry V', in John Drakakis (ed.), *Alternative Shakespeares*, Methuen, 1986.
8 Michael Bogdanov and Joss Buckley, *Shakespeare Lives!: The Taming of the Shrew* and *Timon of Athens*, Channel 4/Quintet Films, 1983, p. 3.
9 Prompt-book of the Royal Shakespeare Company production of *The Taming of the Shrew*, 1978, dir. Michael Bogdanov, in the Shakespeare Centre Library, Stratford-upon-Avon.
10 Irving Wardle, *The Times*, 5 May 1978.
11 Michael Bogdanov interviewed by Christopher J. McCullough in Graham Holderness (ed.), *The Shakespeare Myth*, Manchester University Press, 1988.
12 Robert Cushman, *Observer*, 7 May 1978.
13 Roger Warren, 'A Year of comedies: Stratford 1978', *Shakespeare Survey* 31, 1979, p. 201; Michael Billington, 'A spluttering firework', *Guardian*, 5 May 1978.
14 B. A. Young, *Financial Times*, 5 May 1978.
15 Jane Ellison, 'A win for Kate', *Evening Standard*, 5 May 1978.
16 Benedict Nightingale, 'Wiving it', *New Statesman*, 5 May 1978.
17 Peter Jenkins, 'Macho dreams', *Spectator*, 5 May 1979.
18 Eric Shorter, *Daily Telegraph*, 1 May 1979.
19 Michael Bogdanov, quoted by Michael Billington in 'Why Old Bill needs rejuvenating', *Guardian*, 30 December 1982.
20 Charles Marowitz and Simon Trussler, *Theatre at Work*, Methuen, 1967, p. 170.
21 See Charles Marowitz, *The Marowitz Shakespeare*, Marion Boyars, 1978, pp. 16-18.
22 *Guardian*, 2 November 1973.
23 For this phrase and other production details for *The Shrew* I am indebted to Jinnie Schiele's PhD thesis, 'Post-War Theatre in Camden: a study of three theatre enterprises', 1987; and see Eileen Cottis, Jinnie Schiele and David Hirst, *Charles Marowitz and the Open Space Theatre*, 'Theatre in Focus' series, Chadwick-Healy, forthcoming.

Chapter V

1 Cedric Messina, 'Preface' to The BBC-TV Shakespeare: Richard II, London: BBC, 1978, p. 8.
2 Ann Pasternak Slater, 'An interview with Jonathan Miller', *Quarto*, 10, 1980, p. 9.
3 'Cedric Messina discusses the Shakespeare Plays', *Shakespeare Quarterly*, 30, 1979, p. 137.
4 Stanley Wells, 'A prosaic transformation', *Times Literary Supplement*, 31 October, 1980.
5 John Wilders, 'Introduction' to The BBC-TV Shakespeare: The Taming

   of the Shrew, London: BBC, 1980, p. 8.

6 Jonathan Miller interviewed by Graham Holderness in Holderness (ed.) *The Shakespeare Myth*, Manchester University Press, 1988.

7 Tim Hallinan, 'Jonathan Miller on the Shakespeare plays', *Shakespeare Quarterly*, 32, 1981, p. 134.

8 Sean Day-Lewis, *Daily Telegraph*, 24 October 1980, and Chris Dunkley, 'Taming of the Shrew', *Financial Times*, 24 October 1980.

9 See Stanley Wells, 'Television Shakespeare', *Shakespeare Quarterly*, 33, 1982, p. 268, quoting John Wilders, 'Adjusting the set', *Times Higher Educational Supplement*, 10 July 1981, p. 13.

10 John Naughton, *Observer*, 26 October 1980.

BIBLIOGRAPHY

Texts

The BBC-TV Shakespeare: *The Taming of the Shrew*, London: BBC, 1980.
Geoffrey Bullough, *Narrative and Dramatic Sources of Shakespeare*, Routledge and Kegan Paul, 1957, vol. 1 (*The Taming of a Shrew*).
Richard Hosley, ed., The Pelican Shakespeare: *The Taming of the Shrew*, Harmondsworth: Penguin, 1964, revised 1970.
Brian Morris (ed.), The New Arden Shakespeare: *The Taming of the Shrew*, London: Methuen, 1982.
Ann Thompson, ed., The New Cambridge Shakespeare: *The Taming of the Shrew*, Cambridge University Press, 1984.
James Worsdale, *A Cure for a Scold*, 1735, facsimile, London: Cornmarket Press, 1969.

Criticism

David Addenbrooke, *The Royal Shakespeare Company*, William Kimber, 1974.
Mikhail Bakhtin, *Rabelais and his World*, trans. Helen Iswolsky. Cambridge, Mass.: C.I.T. Press, 1968.
C. L. Barber, *Shakespeare's Festive Comedy*, Princeton University Press, 1959.
John Barton, *Playing Shakespeare*, Methuen, 1986.
Sally Beauman, *The Royal Shakespeare Company: a history of ten decades*, Oxford University Press, 1982.
Catherine Belsey, 'Shakespeare and film', *Literature/Film Quarterly*, XI, Spring 1983, no. 2.
Catherine Belsey, 'Disrupting sexual difference: meaning and gender in the comedies', in John Drakakis (ed.), *Alternative Shakespeares*, London: Methuen, 1986.
Ralph Berry, *On Directing Shakespeare*, Croom Helm, 1977.
Michael Bogdanov and Joss Buckley, *Shakespeare Lives!: The Taming of the Shrew* and *Timon of Athens*, Channel 4/Quintet Films, 1983.
Michael D. Bristol, *Carnival and Theatre*, Methuen, 1985.
Geraldine Cousins, 'The Touring of *The Shrew*' *New Theatre Quarterly*, 2:7, Cambridge University Press, August 1986.
Jonathan Dollimore and Alan Sinfield, 'History and ideology: the instance of *Henry V*', in John Drakakis (ed.), *Alternative Shakespeares*, Methuen, 1986.

Juliet Dusinberre, *Shakespeare and the Nature of Women*, London: Macmillan, 1975.

Phillip Edwards (ed.) *The New Cambridge Shakespeare: Hamlet*, Cambridge University Press, 1985.

John Elsom and Nicholas Tomalin, *The History of the National Theatre*, Jonathan Cape, 1978.

Robert Greene, *The Scottish History of James IV*, ed. Norman Sanders, Methuen, 1970.

Robert Greene (with Thomas Lodge), *A Looking-Glass for London and England*, ed. G. A. Clugston, Garland Publishing, 1980.

Peter Hall, 'A new way with Shakespeare', *Sunday Times*, 22 November 1959.

Peter Hall, 'Shakespeare and the modern director', in *The Royal Shakespeare Company, 1960-1963*, Reinhardt, 1964.

Tim Hallinan, 'Jonathan Miller on the *Shakespeare Plays*', *Shakespeare Quarterley*, 32, 1981.

Tori Haring-Smith, *From Farce to Metadrama: a stage history of 'The Taming of the Shrew', 1594-1983*, Westport, Conn. and London: Greenwood Press, 1985.

Christopher Hill, *The World Turned Upside Down* (1972), Harmondsworth: Penguin, 1975.

Graham Holderness, 'Radical potentiality and institutional closure', in Jonathan Dollimore and Alan Sinfield (eds.), *Political Shakespeare*, Manchester University Press, 1985.

Graham Holderness, *Shakespeare's History*, Dublin: Gill and Macmillan, 1985.

Graham Holderness, *Hamlet*, Milton Keynes: Open University Press, 1987.

Graham Holderness, 'Agincourt 1944: readings in the Shakespeare myth', in Peter Humm, Paul Stigant and Peter Widdowson (eds.), *Popular Fictions*, Methuen, 1987.

Graham Holderness (ed.), *The Shakespeare Myth*, Manchester University Press, 1988.

Graham Holderness, 'The albatross and the swan: two productions at Stratford', *New Theatre Quarterly*, 14, 1988.

Graham Holderness, Nick Potter and John Turner, *Shakespeare: The Plan of History*, London: Macmillan, 1988.

Jack J. Jorgens, *Shakespeare on Film*, Bloomington: Indiana University Press, 1979.

Jan Kott, *Shakespeare Our Contemporary*, 2nd edition, Methuen, 1967.

Thomas Kyd, *The Spanish Tragedy*, ed. Philip Edwards, Manchester University Press, 1977.

Jill L. Levenson, *Shakespeare in Performance: 'Romeo and Juliet*, Manchester University Press, 1987.

Roger Manvell, *Shakespeare and the Film*, South Brunswick and New York: A. S. Barnes, 1971, 1979.

Charles Marowitz, *The Marowitz Shakespeare*, Marion Boyars, 1978.

Charles Marowitz and Simon Trussler, *Theatre at Work*, Methuen, 1967.

Christopher J. McCullough, 'The Cambridge connection: towards a materialist theatre practice', in Graham Holderness (ed.), *The Shakespeare Myth*, Manchester University Press, 1988.

Ann Pasternak Slater, 'An interview with Jonathan Miller', *Quarto*, 10, 1980.

A. P. Rossiter, *English Drama from Early Times to the Elizabethans*, New

York: Barnes and Noble, 1967.

Jinnie Schiele, 'Post-war theatre in Camden: a study of three threatre enterprises', (PhD thesis), North London Polytechnic, 1987.

Alan Sinfield, 'Royal Shakespeare', in Jonathan Dollimore and Alan Sinfield (eds.), *Political Shakespeare*, Manchester University Press, 1985.

Lawrence Stone, *The Family, Sex and Marriage, 1500-1800* (1977), abridged edition, Harmondsworth: Pelican, 1979.

Ann Thompson, '"The warrant of womanhood": Shakespeare and feminist criticism', in Graham Holderness, (ed.), *The Shakespeare Myth*, Manchester University Press, 1988.

Robert Weimann, 'Mimesis in *Hamlet*', in Patricia Parker and Geoffrey Hartmann, (eds.), *Shakespeare and the Question of Theory*, London: Methuen, 1986.

Stanley Wells, 'Television Shakespeare', *Shakespeare Quarterly*, 33, 1982.

John Wilders, 'Adjusting the set', *Times Higher Educational Supplement*, 10 July 1981.

CASTLISTS OF MAJOR CHARACTERS IN PRODUCTIONS DISCUSSED

John Barton (1960)

Christopher Sly	Jack MacGowran	*Gremio*	Ian Holm
Hostess	Mavis Edwards	*Hortensio*	Tony Church
Lord	Ian Richardson	*Biondello*	Dinsdale Landen
Lucentio	Peter Jeffrey	*Petruchio*	Peter O'Toole
Tranio	James Bree	*Grumio*	Patrick Wymark
Baptista	Paul Hardwick	*Pedant*	Donald Layne-Smith
Katharina	Peggy Ashcroft	*Tailor*	Clifford Rose
Bianca	Elizabeth Sellars	*Vincentio*	Roy Dotrice

Franco Zeffirelli (1966)

Lucentio	Michael York	*Biondello*	Roy Holder
Tranio	Alfred Lynch	*Petruchio*	Richard Burton
Baptista	Michael Hordern	*Grumio*	Cyril Cusack
Katharina	Elizabeth Taylor	*Pedant*	Vernon Dobtcheff
Bianca	Natasha Pyne	*Tailor*	Ken Parry
Gremio	Alan Webb	*Vincentio*	Mark Dignam

Michael Bogdanov (1978)

Christopher Sly/ Petruchio	Jonathan Pryce	*Gremio*	Paul Webster
		Biondello	Allan Hendrick
Hostess/ Katharina	Paola Dionisotti	*Grumio*	David Suchet
		Pedant	Geoffrey Freshwater
Lucentio	Anthony Higgins	*Tailor*	Conrad Asquith
Tranio	Ian Charleson	*Vincentio*	George Raistrick
Lord/Baptista	Paul Brooke		
Bianca	Zoë Wanamaker		

Jonathan Miller (1980)

Lucentio	Simon Chandler	*Biondello*	Harry Waters
Tranio	Anthony Pedley	*Petruchio*	John Cleese
Baptista	John Franklyn-Robbins	*Grumio*	David Kincaid
		Pedant	John Bird
Katharina	Sarah Badel	*Tailor*	Alan Hay
Bianca	Susan Penhaligon	*Vincentio*	John Barron
Gremio	Frank Thornton		

INDEX